T0146702

Hello, My Sweetheart

Hello, My Sweetheart

A Life and Career on Three Continents

SIGRID GASSNER-ROBERTS

HELLO, MY SWEETHEART
A LIFE AND CAREER ON THREE CONTINENTS

iUniverse books may be ordered through booksellers or by contacting:

iUniverse
1663 Liberty Drive
Bloomington, IN 47403
www.iuniverse.com
1-800-Authors (1-800-288-4677)

ISBN: 978-1-5320-0193-2 (sc)
ISBN: 978-1-5320-0192-5 (e)

Library of Congress Control Number: 2016911929

Print information available on the last page.

iUniverse rev. date: 08/05/2016

Hello, sweetheart,

You left me while I was not at home. Why did you not wait for me to come home? I asked you to wait, but, at the same time, I released you from my care. I set you free. Still, when I came home and found you gone, an emptiness overcame me, and I felt drained. In many ways, you gave me strength and courage to handle our lives. Now I am alone. You are not there to listen to me. No longer can I bring the outside world into our living room and tell you all about it. For many years you asked me every day, "How were your students?" You still asked me that question long after I had retired. Whenever I was out, you assumed that I was in the university teaching my students or attending a meeting. I always gave you a kiss, and you answered with a smooch. These wonderful moments of closeness are gone forever …

Sweetheart, I feel I must think back and contemplate our time together—more so, relive our life together. I don't want to lose you from my memory, my heart. As the hotel security guard Sabri in Tunisia said to me, "He has not died; he is with God and lives in your heart." He consoled me with his words while tears were streaming down my face and my heart was shaking. Yes, you are living in my heart, day in, day out. Often during the course of a day, I talk to you and ask, "What do you say to that? How would you handle this situation, sweetheart?" I learned so much from you. However, I learned most during the thirty-two years of your illness. Looking after you and fulfilling my duties at the university were a huge challenge.

*****

I cannot forget, nor do I want to forget, that thirtieth of January 1980 at Hanny and Mario's in Vienna, when you picked up the Biedermeier teapot after dinner and said, admiringly, "Is this not a beautiful teapot!" Then you placed it back on the table and murmured, *"Mein Kopf ...* is getting bigger" and collapsed into my arms. I yelled for Mario, who was on the phone to order a taxi to take us to the airport, and said, "Mario, we don't need a taxi; we need an ambulance. Lloyd is having a stroke!" It was shortly before eight in the evening.

It was, and still is, the worst shock of my life. Within seconds, I lost you as I had known you for only four years. I remember every minute of that night of the thirtieth of January 1980. The ambulance arrived and took you to the AKH (Allgemeines Krankenhaus), the largest and most prestigious hospital in Vienna. The hassles we had in the outpatients division were unbelievable. It was the first time I had to put my foot down and fight for you and demand that you be seen by a senior doctor "who knew what he was talking about." I had hardly finished my sentence, when Dozent Marmolis entered the room, gave you one look, and demanded that a CT (computed tomography) be done. The first set of doctors had guessed that you probably had an epileptic fit or a heart problem. Meanwhile, I was sent to the admissions office, where I encountered more problems. As we were foreigners with travel insurance, I was asked to put down thirty thousand shillings. Where should I take that money from? We were on our way back home to Australia! Thank goodness financially well-to-do friends were waiting for us in the lounge of Qantas Airlines at the Vienna Airport. Of course, any title, be it an academic one or one awarded by business or politics, was and still is of advantage in Vienna. So I made use of it and asked to speak to Dr. Peter Steidl, the then Austrian honorary consul to South Australia and a colleague of mine at the university, who was with his family in the business lounge. I told him what had happened. A few nights prior to that life-changing event, we had had dinner at that family's home. I remember very well how the consul's father had admired your fitness and envied your strength and commitment to look after your health by doing physical exercises for years, first at Gyula's gym and later at the gym of my university. The consul's father asked me what help I needed—thirty thousand shillings. He spoke to the relevant person in that admissions office, and all I heard was "Ja, Herr Kommerzialrat, natürlich, Herr Kommerzialrat …" He brought the money to the hospital the next day at eleven in the morning. How lucky we were to know these people and find them so helpful! What would someone have done who did not know a rich person in Vienna? I had been told that you could not be admitted to the AKH without the prepayment. By the time I returned from that office, your CT had been done, and you were about to be wheeled into your room. I stayed with you until past midnight, when Mario came to take me back to his house.

I was emotionally paralyzed, but my brain became very active. That same night, I rang your brother Jared in the United States and my sisters in Vorarlberg. Jared—a veteran of World War II and, as a consequence, mentally impaired, devoid of empathy, but very rational—told me that he would not come to Vienna; instead he would send me $5,000 to help take care of bills, and if I wanted more, I would have to pay that back. My sister Ruth jumped onto the next train and came to assist me emotionally and to see you, my sweetheart.

The next morning, Professor Reisner examined you and then spoke to me in detail about your condition. He showed me the computer images, pronounced the diagnosis—a subarachnoid aneurysm of the communicating artery—and explained the course of medical treatment. The bleeding in your brain needed to subside, and the artery had to be clipped where it had burst. The operation could not be performed before the fifth day after the rupture, but it had to be done before the ninth day. I sat with you every day from eight in the morning to ten at night, when the staff asked me to leave. Every morning at nine, Professor Reisner visited you and shared his observations with me. He always arrived with a group of aspiring neurologists, sometimes up to fifteen young doctors. When he wanted you to "wake up"—you seemed not to respond when the doctors were with you—Professor Reisner called me to reenter the room and "wake you up." Every time you opened your eyes and smiled when I touched you and kissed you and quietly spoke to you. And every time, Professor Reisner said, looking at his young doctors, "Das kann nur die Liebe einer Frau." His words strengthened me in my resolve to help you as best I could.

Then came the morning of the fourth of February, the fifth day after the insult to your brain. You were transferred from neurology to neurosurgery and became a patient of Professor Koos. My youngest sister, Annelies, arrived. Ruth had had to go back home to her teaching position. Midmorning a nurse took you to the neurosurgical wing, and I followed you. You were put into a private single room.

Annelies joined us with a box full of tasty open sandwiches—I can still smell them as I think of that time. I could not share these delicacies with you, as you were deeply unconscious. It was the first food I actually remember. What I ate on all the other days, I cannot recall. In the afternoon, a nurse came and told me that Professor Koos was on his way to visit you to decide and discuss further medical procedures. He had studied the previous test results, checked you over, and then, looking at me, said rather despairingly, "If I operate on him now, he will die, and if I don't, he will die within twenty-four hours. What shall I do?" We looked at each other, then at you, my dear, lying still and hardly breathing. My heart was heavy; I felt almost numb, but then I told him clearly, "Do what you think is right, I shall accept the result." Professor Koos nodded, got up, and left the room, and a nurse entered. About an hour or two later, I was called to the nurses' phone. Professor Koos informed me that he had made the following decisions: a private nurse would come shortly and observe you, my sweetheart, and check all functions needed for your survival of the operation. He would stay in his office all night, if necessary, until the moment arrived that you had even a minimal chance to survive the operation, for at that particular moment, you did not have a chance at all. I agreed and thanked him and repeated my resolve to accept the result.

The private nurse was not happy with my presence and urged me to go to my temporary home at Mario and Hanny's. Annelies and I had a meal there and then retired for the night. Annelies lay down on a sofa—she had traveled for eight hours coming from Bludenz to Vienna (these days, trains are much faster)—while I sat fully dressed in an old-fashioned fauteuil with a high back, resting, but fully alert in case the hospital wanted to contact me—and ready to run there. I prayed for you, sweetheart, and as a good Catholic, put everything into God's hands.

I probably dozed off a few times. However, at a quarter after four in the morning, I felt a strong urge to go and see you. I abruptly jumped up, grabbed my spring coat (after all, we don't need a winter coat in Adelaide) and ran to the AKH. As I reached your room, you were just being wheeled out of it, heading to the operating theater. I held your hand all the way and made a cross on your forehead and kissed you when we reached the door to the OP theater. I saw you being wheeled into an x-ray room for a lung x-ray. Then the doors were closed behind you. I felt as if I was made of stone. I was neither sad nor desperate; I did not cry. Professor Koos and I had briefly looked at each other and bowed our heads, and then I turned around ready to leave. Thank goodness, Annelies had just arrived. We began meandering in icy-cold Vienna, a city still devoid of people and cars, not even a streetcar anywhere. At six, we noticed a café opening. Freezing as we were, we entered and warmed ourselves with a cup of coffee. We did not talk much. Each of us was caught in her own thoughts. By the time we left the café, Vienna had woken up, and people were heading toward work. Trams were running, bakeries opened up, and eventually daylight crept over the city. At eight, Annelies suggested ringing the hospital to ask how the operation was proceeding. I was told it would take many hours. We went on walking again, but I tell you, my dear sweetheart, I do not remember where to. All I remember is that it was freezing cold, and we drank tea in a number of cafés. At ten o'clock,

I called the hospital again, and again I was informed that the operation was still going on and would still take a long time. Annelies reminded me that that was actually good news: Sweetheart, you were still alive! We finally returned to Hanny and Mario's to warm up. Walking in the cold was probably much better than sitting in a cozy room worrying and being restless. I was sure my sister Irene spent hours in her convent chapel in Salzburg praying for you, as did many other nuns as well. They all liked you. I still have the drawing one of the sisters made for us and gave us when we visited the Nonnberg Abbey on our honeymoon. "God's will be done," they will have prayed. By about midday, I phoned the hospital again … Operation still going on … At one thirty, I was told that the operation was a success, and you were being transferred to the recovery room. What a relief! At that point I did not think about anything else. You were alive, and that was all that counted. Nobody around me mentioned anything about the condition you might be in or the deficiencies you might have now—after all you had had very serious **brain surgery.**

The next morning, I rang the recovery room doctor and asked about you. She told me that you had died during the night. What a shock that was! I immediately called Professor Reisner, who knew nothing about it. We went to the section of the AKH where you were supposed to be. It turned out that the doctor on duty had made a mistake; you were alive, but the patient whose brain was operated on after you, also an American, had died. This mistake had severe consequences for the doctor on duty. I was told to come back at one thirty in the afternoon, when I was allowed to see you. Upon arrival, I had to put on a green coat and cap and cover my shoes with plastic. Upon seeing a number of people, all unconscious with all sorts of drips leading into their bodies, I was about to faint. The doctor on duty yelled at me, "Pull yourself together; this way, you are of no help to your husband!" He brought me a chair and a glass of water and told me to talk to you, dear. What was the sense of talking to you lying in a coma on a bed? He told me that your subconscious mind would hear me. So I began to remind you of our first date.

*****

I remember that day in 1975 after we had met at Karin and Mike's on the Fourth of July. We drove up to Cleland Park on that Sunday afternoon. I remember you talking about the immense importance of the human brain: what it could do, how it could be misused by brainwashing, and so on. You spoke of hypnotherapy, of Bryan, of transactional analysis, and many other fascinating aspects of psychology. I was amazed at your interests and your knowledge and very happy about it all. But then, four and a half years later, this wonderful brain of yours had to suffer such a terrible assault due to a burst aneurysm in a very unfortunate part of your brain! There is no point in asking why or why you. It has happened; it is part of life. There is no answer to that anyway, so why ask the question?

*****

The day we met for the first time is as vivid in my mind as the day I nearly lost you. Karin, one of my students, insisted that I should meet you, a very nice American, a business friend of her husband, Mike. I did not want to go on a blind date, and so I decided to stay at home. I had just returned from three days in the Riverland, where I had visited the matriculation classes in Waikerie, Berry, Loxton, and Glossop. In those days I was the liaison officer between the German Department of the University of Adelaide and those high schools where German was taught. This means that in addition to being a lecturer at the university, I had the responsibilities of a chief examiner of German at the South Australian Public Examinations Board. The head of our department was Professor Brian Coghlan, who had initially appointed me to lecture at the university in 1974. I did not know that Karin had also invited him and his wife Sybil along with another seven friends. When I did not arrive at that Fourth of July party, Mike came to get me. All in all, we were twelve people around an oval-shaped dining room table. Due to my lateness, I had missed out on cocktails and the introduction to you and all the other guests. My place was next to Mike, while you sat next to Karin; in other words we sat on opposite sides of this oval-shaped table, and therefore had no chance to talk to each other. I cast my eyes every so often at you with some curiosity; however, our eyes never met.

After a long, delicious, sit-down dinner with five courses, we finally moved to our hosts' beautiful garden to admire its layout and plants and furniture. Still, you and I had not met formally. I talked to every other guest but you, realizing that you had to be a very well-brought-up man, because you did not push but waited for the right moment to introduce yourself. Around midnight, Mike began to work on a barbecue—and that after a five-course dinner!

Karin brought me a large potato on a plate, telling me where to choose the meat. I looked at the potato thinking that I could not possibly eat it all. As I lifted my eyes, you stood in front of me, smiling. Not giving you a chance to say anything, which was actually bad mannered, my first words to you were, "Would you share this potato with me?" And it became a lifetime. By one thirty in the morning, I was tired and wanted to go home. The person who was supposed to take me home was beyond driving, I thought, and therefore I asked Karin to get me a taxi. You heard that and offered to drive me home, as you were a teetotaler. At my front door, you asked me for a date on that weekend, but I refused, giving lots of excuses. While you were driving me home, I had asked myself, "Do I want to get involved with this man? Why should I want to get involved, since my life as a single and very independent woman had been quite good? Do I want to burden myself with further responsibilities? Had I not been happy so far? Do I need a relationship at forty-one years of age? Do I miss something in this life?" The answer to all these questions was "Not really. Why should I want to change my life?" I could not see a good reason to change. I had never wanted children and at forty-one, I was too old for that anyway. As I continued to say no to any suggested date for a get-together that week or in the following week, you asked for my telephone number. I was tired and gave you my number and a time to ring me—on Sunday between six and seven in the evening.

On Saturday of that weekend, I walked with Lotte, a Jewish friend in her late seventies, along one of the beaches. At one point I mentioned having met you at a Fourth of July party. She was the wife of a psychologist and had studied, but never practiced, psychology herself. I noticed her becoming quite interested in my refusal to meet you again and asked me to ring her if I changed my mind. Obviously she did not quite trust my decision. You rang me at the given time, but I did not answer the phone. You rang me every ten minutes, but still I did not answer. You rang the last time at seven in the evening, but I did not pick up the receiver. Okay, that's it; I can continue to be free and independent. Little did I know about you! On Monday morning, my phone rang in my office shortly before nine. Of course, I had to take the call. Lord behold, it was you, sweetheart! You simply wanted to meet me again sometime during that week. I learned how persistent you could be when you wanted something! So we agreed on Thursday. Why Thursday and not any other day? A silly reason had flashed through my mind. Thursday is/was Stubatetag in Vorarlberg. That means the day when boys visit girls in my home state in Austria! I knew that from experience, but I had never on those occasions met anybody I was interested in while young. So it was a silly notion to meet you exactly on that day. Or had I already come to a decision subconsciously about you? Anyway, we met on that day.

On Thursday, you picked me up at my flat, and we drove to Los Amigos in Rundle Mall. We had a nice Spanish dinner. I was happy about your choice of restaurant and food, because it showed me that you were open-minded. You mentioned your years in the United States and your involvement in World War II and the Korean War, and I mentioned my eight years in New York, my relatives in Wisconsin, and my visits to the Midwest. I marveled at the American log cabins I had seen in Wisconsin. While I was describing those cabins, you took a biro and your napkin and drew such a cabin on it. You handed it to me saying, "I'd like to build such a cabin for you in Wisconsin or anywhere else." I could not believe what I was hearing; I was stunned. At that moment, I knew that you and I were made for each other. I knew then that it had to be that we would meet, call it fate, or Fügung. I had never met a man who would have built anything for me, who had understood me and been prepared to fulfill my wishes so unconditionally. I knew then that we would share our lives together. Sweetheart, as I am retelling this story to you, I still see us sitting in that restaurant, and you drawing the log cabin and explaining to me precisely how you would build it and why that way and not another way. You won my heart right there and then. You drove me back to my flat with my promise to meet you again on Sunday for a drive to Cleland Park.

We met twice a week in the following three weeks before I had to go to America and Europe to speak at conferences. I was chatting with some friends at the airport, when you arrived to see me off. I asked all of them what I should bring them. Each one had a wish; only you said nothing. When I asked you, you answered, "Nothing; just come home safely." Again you surprised me. While I was in my hometown, Brian Coghlan visited me and my family for a few days. We were having lunch—apricot dumplings—when the postman rang the doorbell and handed me a small yellow package. After the meal, my father wanted to know who had sent it to me and what was in it. I found your letter, a blue piece of paper, and a rough opal. You gave me a description of the opal and wrote a factual, unemotional letter. At the end it said that you wanted to know the date and time of my return, and you wished me a good flight. My father wanted to have a close look at your letter. I did not want him to see it, so I said, "Dad, it is written in English and in an American handwriting, so you won't understand anything at all." At that moment I had forgotten that my father had studied graphology while at the School of Fine Arts in Vienna. He obviously wanted to interpret your handwriting. I gave him the letter, and everybody around the table was curious. I remember vividly how my dad kept saying "ah" and "oh" and how he moved the letter in his hands to get the right light. Finally he put it down, looked at me very earnestly, and said, "Child, he is serious." I was stunned. Brian exclaimed that he had met you about two hours earlier than me, because he had been in time for cocktails at that Fourth of July party. I asked Dad for an analysis of your handwriting, which he willingly provided. We were all surprised at what we heard. Brian was the first to speak by expressing that what Dad had said was exactly how he had perceived you at that party at Karin and Mike's: honest, serious, highly intelligent, introverted, and so forth, and a man who had had a difficult life and suffered a lot. How right Dad was I found out in due course. Little by little you told me about much of the sufferings and pain in your life. Before I flew back to Australia, I asked my younger sister Ruth—she was weeding in the garden at the time— what she would say if I married you. She looked up at me and answered, "I would be happy for you."

*****

As promised in your blue letter, you picked me up at the airport. On the way to my apartment in Glenunga, you asked me to marry you. I got a shock! Please, give me some time; we have only known each other for a few weeks! The Sunday after my return, I invited you to lunch. I served a typically Austrian meal, pork roast with bread dumplings and red cabbage. You complimented me on my cooking by saying, "I did not expect an academic to be able to cook so well." I was happy and decided to repeat luncheon invitations on weekends. The time came to take you to the Austrian Club in Ovingham and to introduce you to some close friends. It seemed to me that a new world had opened up for you. One day in October, you suggested we visit my cousin Hans and his son, Raimund, in Melbourne. On the way, between Naracoort and Bordertown, you stopped the car and proposed to me. For the rest of our lives together I teased you about that because we were in the middle of the "little desert." I often joked by saying that I only said yes to you because you might have left me standing there had I not accepted. You reached into your trouser pockets and pulled out two wedding rings with the date engraved, 10-10-1975 LGR on one ring and 10-10-1975 SNG on the other. How could you be so certain that I would say yes? We celebrated our engagement in the Cuckoo in the Dandenongs.

You realized that I got "cold feet" after the engagement. We had a great time getting to know each other better and finding out about each other's past. You wanted me to have a long talk with Bryan, your hypnotherapist and close friend. We met in a hotel on North Terrace to discuss your past experiences, many of them having been traumatic. He told me that you needed a lot of patience and love to come to terms with many unfortunate happenings in your life. Most importantly, you were in need of understanding and security. You had lost so much in your life: your mother through a car accident at the age of twelve; the love of your father soon after, because he could not cope with your high intellect (IQ of 138) and your independence and resourcefulness; and very many of your friends and mates in the US Navy. You often told me of the initial landing on Guadalcanal, the largest of the Solomon Islands, when forty-eight of you Navy boys—you were attached to the Marines then—landed, and only seven of you walked off, as you used to say. The rest lost their lives either in battle or through malaria. You often told me that you were afraid of getting close to someone, because whomever you had gotten close to, you lost sooner or later. Bryan and I discussed these experiences in your life in great detail. I decided there and then never to leave you, to make up for all your losses as best I could. We promised each other never to do anything or go anywhere without the other. This, of course, turned out to be irrational, and therefore impossible to live up to. I realized that when I had to attend a meeting of the Goethe Society, while you were sitting in the car waiting for me for over two hours. So we excluded job-related occasions.

One day I went to David Jones after work to buy a dress. I had told you about my plan but did not think about telling you exactly when I would go to that department store. Suddenly you appeared. I had tried three dresses on and just made up my mind which one I would buy, when you interfered and told the saleswoman to show you where the dresses of my size were. A while later you returned with a rack full of dresses to try on. I was shocked! You asked me to try each one of them on and show myself to you wearing it. We ended up buying three (!) dresses. That was the beginning of our couch sessions, as I called them. For me, it was a big thing not to be able to buy my own clothes alone. My independence was encroached upon, restrained. I felt quite disturbed, unhappy, and uneasy. There was a great need to discuss this incident before it became a problem. You saw it as a possible sign of our drifting apart. For me it was a sign of you wanting to dominate me. I won this argument, but our discussion had made me very aware of your fear of losing me and of your desire to be involved in any decision making. In the course of the next two years, I became much more careful in talking to you—never to "run over you," always to include you in any conversation. It was good to have learned that early in our relationship, as it became immensely important in the long years of your illness. You hated it when people around you spoke anything but English, because you felt left out. So all my married life, I translated or passed on to you the gist of what had been said. You were not a person that could be sidelined. Your physique was strong and impressive not only due to your size (six feet four) and your handsomeness, but also due to the strength of your character and the way you carried yourself. Your training at the US Naval Academy followed by eight years in the navy and later on your time in the coast guard as well as in the merchant navy had left their marks on your body: strong, straight, and powerful.

I mentioned our couch sessions. They were enormously useful in getting to know you and myself. You were so clever and knew so much about cementing our relationship, showing me my shortcomings as far as our relationship was concerned, as I had been living an independent life up to the day I met you. In a most gentle and understanding way, you made me aware of the things I did and said that you did not like, so that I could never be angry with you. Even the introduction to our sessions amazed me. You began by inviting me to sit on the couch with you after dinner; you held my hand and started talking by saying, "Sweetheart, I have a bad feeling today. Could it be that you said or did something that gave me that feeling? Let's talk about the day." So we went over the happenings of that day, starting with breakfast, then the drive to university, where you dropped me off on days when you did not go to your gym first to do some weight lifting, and then lunch together on the banks of the river Torrens. You came home from your office at about six in the evening. You made me aware of brushing you off when I was doing university work, and you wanted to ask me something, or when I made a rather thoughtless comment on something that was important to you but unimportant to me, or when I was "short and snappy" and refused to beat about the bush and came to the point without giving much or any consideration of another point of view. In all fairness, I could never be angry at you for showing me myself in your mirror, because you were always right. Within months, I noticeably changed. I had begun to realize that you were not my student but my partner.

*****

We got married on the twenty-ninth of November 1976.

Our honeymoon took us first to my home in Austria and to Bangkok on the way back to Australia. We arrived in Bludenz on the eighteenth of December. Egmont, Annelies's husband, and their son, Martin, met us at Zurich airport.

Martin, then about eight years old, munching a roll with chocolate in it, offered you a bite, a first welcome into my family. I do not remember whether we stopped at Annelies's home first to meet her and their younger son Wolfram before driving on to Bludenz to meet my parents and Ruth, or whether we carried on to Bludenz straight away. In any case, your arrival was expected with great curiosity and interest. You won the hearts and minds of my family and relatives in no time. At Christmas, we rang my sister Irene (Sister Andrea, OSB) at the convent Nonnberg in Salzburg. She asked Dad what he thought of you. Dad expressed his happiness with you, and she commented, "How can you say that, as you cannot communicate with him?" Dad answered, "Between Lloyd and me, words are superfluous." It was true; you and Dad sat in the living room holding hands and often looked at each other. You and my dad seemed to have a perfect understanding without ever saying a word to each other. Later on, you often told me that you wanted to be buried next to him. I did just that.

We stayed in my upstairs apartment and took our meals with the family. We came downstairs after my aging parents had been prepared for breakfast. Both of them were in their eighties and unwell. Dad had had a stroke, and due to heart problems, he had been given a pacemaker. Mother had dementia and did not talk anymore. Neither of them had been outside of the house for quite some time. Ruth and an elderly woman were looking after them. You called the woman "Gott im Himmel," because that is what she said anytime there was a problem. Ruth needed her help because she had to teach in Bürs, a neighboring village. She was a member of a lay order of the Catholic Church called the Sisters of Good Tidings (Schwestern der Frohbotschaft). Every morning when we came to breakfast, you greeted my mum saying, "I love you," touching her hands. She answered with a smile and looked at you full of good feelings for you. Ruth told me once we were back in Australia that she kept looking at the kitchen door for quite some time after our departure expecting you and your greetings. Gradually she ceased doing it and withdrew again into herself.

On Boxing Day, you suggested we should take Dad out and walk with him to a café. Dad was very happy. He managed to walk from one café to the next until we found one open. The owner was most surprised to see us and immediately found a table for us. Dad introduced you to him and then showed you all the rooms and the antiques he had restored and sold to the owner over time. He was so proud of you that he wanted everybody in the place to know you. As was his habit in his healthy days, he bought a slice of cake each for Mum and Ruth, before we walked home.

On a sunny day about a week later, we took Mum out in a wheelchair. As we passed the home of her best girlfriend from her schooldays, her friend sitting by the window noticed us and waved. Mum's happiness was written all over her face. She even managed to say "Marie," her friend's name. We could not take her to a café because in those days no provisions existed for disabled persons to enter cafés in Bludenz.

I remember attending midnight Mass in the Holy Cross Church in Bludenz with you. It used to be the one occasion when most townspeople went to church. As I had been a teacher in our town for a number of years, I knew many of the people we met. You stood out among the crowd due to your size and looks. I noticed surprised, admiring, and envious glances from many who saw us. Later I was asked by numerous of my closer friends, where I had found you! I was very proud of you!

On the twentieth of January 1977, we left for Adelaide via Bangkok. It was difficult to leave because of my aging parents. We never saw them again. Our honeymoon in Bangkok had a peculiar beginning, as our luggage went to Hong Kong. Swiss Air was good enough to give us money and provide us with a taxi to go shopping in a large department store. We spent five days in that city and its surroundings, taking tours and exploring the center. It became the first of several visits to that interesting, bustling place. We used it as a stopover on future visits to Austria.

*****

In May 1978, we traveled to the United States on the way to Europe. It was my first study leave granted by my university. For you, it was the first time to visit your home country since the Korean War. After a short work-related stop in Honolulu, Hawaii, and one in Los Angeles, California, we were ready to head for Mammoth Lakes in the Sierra Nevada, where your brother Jared lived. He met us at the airport in Los Angeles and took us in his car to his home in the mountains. It had been my wish to drive through the desert. Along the way, we spent a night at the air force base—your brother had been in the air force during World War II—where we got inexpensive accommodation for one night. I had never been on a military base and was fascinated by the atmosphere and the hustle and bustle there. The next morning, we drove on to Mammoth Lakes to spend a few days with Jared. I remember climbing up a mountain and passing guesthouses named Arlberg and Tyrol and felt almost like being home. It was a skiing area where Austrian skiing instructors worked during the winter season. Jared told us that he worked there during the winter doing all sorts of chores including shoveling snow and helping skiers with their equipment. In summer, he managed Lake Convict nearby and its boat rental to tourists. He told us that since his plane crash had left him with a mental problem, he could not take any inside job. He could only work outdoors. He had become an outdoor man, most interested in nature, animals, traveling in motor homes, and visiting foreign lands. As soon as you and Jared talked about your childhood and teenage years, you got into strife because of your different recollections.

Jared was five years old, and you were twelve, when you lost your mother in a car accident caused by a drunken driver. Your sister Glenn (or Sis, as you called her later) was three at that time. You had become too difficult to handle, you told me, so your father sent you off to boarding schools. It seems you were a genius in thinking up boyhood pranks that angered many adults around you. Your mother always stood up for you, but your father, an MIT (Massachusetts Institute of Technology) graduate must have been a very strict parent belonging to the upper middle class of Boston. His own father, George Litch Roberts, a famous Boston lawyer specializing in patent law, looks just as serious and stern and commanding on his photographs as your father, Harold Barnes Roberts. Your father had his offices in Manhattan and was involved in the erection of many buildings there. Your grandfather's autobiography is a meticulously written account not only of his life but also of the life of the upper classes in Boston at that time, about 150 years ago. He passed away in 1934 at the age of ninety-four years, having gone to his office until he was ninety. His elder son, Odin, your uncle, a partner in your grandfather's law firm, died in his early sixties. We found out a lot more about your family a year later, when we visited your cousins in Stanford, California, and in Boston.

We left Mammoth Lakes by a small airplane and visited Tucson, Arizona, because I had some academic work to do there. Against our wishes, Jared had notified Sis about our visiting Tucson, the town where she lived with her husband, Hal, and their son, Harold. You had not had any contact with Sis for about sixteen years. You had been in touch with Jared off and on. He had even visited you a couple of times in Adelaide. As you had not been in the United States since the early fifties, you told me it was time to catch up with your family. We were among the last passengers to enter the arrivals hall in Tucson. You headed to the counter to reconfirm our onward flight when a small but strong woman walked up to you and said, "You must be my brother; you walk like my father." I was amazed. She insisted we stay with her in her home and not in the Hilton Hotel, where we were booked to spend the next two nights. I wanted to see the huge cacti in the desert, so she drove us there before we went to her home. Her husband, Hal, was waiting for us in the house. It was not a successful visit after so many years because Sis talked of little else but your ruining her dolls and other playthings. Hal sat in the kitchen drinking beer. He asked me, "What do you want from us?" My answer was "Nothing at all." The next morning she took us to the State University of Arizona, where I had a conference with colleagues who were also researching brain-compatible learning, while you spent time with your sister. In the evening, we had dinner in a hotel with Sis, Hal, their son, Harold, and Jared's son, Scott. I was somewhat annoyed at you because when the waitress arrived to take the orders you said, "Order what you want; money is no object." There my Alemannic trait—not wasting money—showed, for money *is* always an object. I still think you just wanted to show off a bit.

With a copy of your grandfather's autobiography in the suitcase, we left for New York. Initially we stayed with Carol and Al on Staten Island. You were busy reading your grandfather's book, while I was involved in academic work. In the autobiography, you found information that led you to locate the one and only friend of your youth, John Berger, at that time living in New Jersey. You were most excited when he and his wife invited us to visit them in Cherry Hills and spend the night there. When I heard that he had become a lawyer, I took the opportunity to learn how we had to go about finding out your correct date of birth. Your documents showed three different birth years: 1921, 1922, and 1923. You had a delayed birth certificate dated 1921, a corrected delayed birth certificate dated 1922, and a document with the year of your birth given as 1923. I wanted this settled once and for all. How important this would become at the time of your death, I could not foresee. I was very happy that you could catch up with your friend John and was very sad when his wife wrote to us about his death six months later. He had been suffering from cancer when we were visiting.

Carol and her husband, Al, living on Staten Island, New York, surprised us with a wonderful party, having invited friends from the island and colleagues from Wagner College, where I had lived and worked from 1966 to 1968. It was great to see them all again, reminisce about old times, eat, drink, and dance on Carol and Al's lawn. We stayed for two nights and then moved on to Manhattan to work at the public library and at the City University of New York. The rest of our time we spent with Frances and Alex Godwin, who lived on Madison Avenue. Frances and Alex had become my second sponsors during my time as a Fulbright Scholar. My first sponsors were the Pierpont Morgan family, friends of Governor Nelson Rockefeller, during my first Fulbright year. I was very lucky with my sponsors. Living on Staten Island, it took me two hours to get from Wagner College to Hunter College: two buses on the island, then the Staten Island Ferry, followed by two subways, and the same way back again. It was not only time-consuming; it was also dangerous on the way back in the night. The Fulbright Commission gave all Fulbright recipients "a shoulder to cry on," as they called it. It was a very good idea because one can feel extremely lonely even in a huge city like New York. One needs good advice, sometimes help, and a place to go to, when things get tough. One day when I had a bad cold and needed a doctor, Mrs. Pierpont Morgan was most generous and sent a taxi to Wagner College to pick me up and bring me to her doctor in Manhattan. After the consultation, I had dinner with her and her son in their home, my first introduction to "how the other half lives." It was in many ways an eye-opener. Little did I know what more was to come. Needless to say, Mrs. Pierpont Morgan paid the doctor's bill. At that point I did not expect my scholarship to be extended for another year.

*****

Toward the end of the first year, the Institute of International Education, situated opposite the UN Building at the East River, invited all Fulbright students in New York to a meeting with our sponsors. The purpose was, of course, fund-raising. I was invited to give a talk on racial problems in New York. Remember, Lloyd, I told you that after I had applied for a Fulbright Scholarship, I was asked about racial tensions in the United States in my oral exam. I could not have answered that question with the understanding and frankness I showed, had I not lived in a black American family in Chicago for four days in August 1963. In that year, I had applied for a visa for three months to live and work in America for eight weeks as an international camp counselor. We were 126 young Europeans who wanted to go to the United States at low cost. I worked in a Jewish camp (Camp Willoway) in the Pocono Mountains and had most interesting experiences; for example, how to survive in a forest without food and matches to make a fire, how to build a float, and how to make enamel jewelry. I learned to eat kosher food and took part in Friday evening predinner ceremonies. Every Saturday, we watched a film about the persecution of the Jewish people throughout history, and films such as *The Diary of Ann Frank*, *The Nuremberg Trial*, and films about the horrors of life and death in concentration camps. To me, living and working in that camp was an immensely important learning experience. Our pay was a three-week trip to an area of our choice—we were given three areas to choose from. I chose Chicago; St. Louis; Georgia; West Virginia; Washington, DC; and Philadelphia. In Chicago, three of us camp counselors were boarded by a black middle-class family. Their children and friends had just returned from Martin Luther King's march to Washington. We were asked if we wanted to go with them to a meeting to be held in somebody's cellar to discuss the march and King's famous "I have a dream" speech. I was thrilled to go, but one of us was scared. It became one of the most fascinating evenings in my life. We ate potato chips and salt crackers, and drank buckets of horrible red Kool-Aid without soda in it. I remember these young black Americans being full of enthusiasm and hope and plans for themselves and their country. It was the most exhilarating atmosphere I have ever experienced. The atmosphere was contagious. I found myself laughing and clapping my hands and singing Peter, Paul, and Mary songs, which I knew from my weeks in the Jewish camp. The participants spoke of their experiences at the Washington march and the mood it had created among the marchers. We stayed together until the early morning hours and finally left singing "We Shall Overcome."

Of course, this tremendous event helped me a great deal in preparing my talk to the Fulbright sponsors. I spoke of that march: of the importance of education in the context of integration, acceptance, and equality, none of which could be achieved in a short time; of striding toward it day by day; and of Abraham Lincoln and his words "All men are created equal." Some of the enthusiasm of my night with the marchers must have spilled over to that meeting of the sponsors, for I received a lot of applause and, more importantly for me, a second year of the Fulbright Scholarship.

*****

Sweetheart, we often talked of my years in America: the experiences I had, good or bad; the people I met; and the students I taught. Those were very important years in my life. My year in Birmingham and London (August 1958 to September 1959) was also important in my development, but not nearly as much as my eight years in New York. When I told you about my experiences in England, you were shocked at the way I was treated in Birmingham by my employer's wife. I had met her and her husband in Lech, a world-famous Austrian skiing resort on the Arlberg Mountain. They were looking for someone to care for their three boys, aged two, three, and five years, and generally to look after their household. I had already been teaching in Vorarlberg for four years, when I asked for a year's unpaid leave to study English in England. As leave was granted, I took on the job and traveled to Birmingham, much to the chagrin of my mother. She was like a mother hen, always worried about her four daughters. My stay with these nouveaux riche people was most disappointing, so I left for London after seven weeks. At that time, about ten thousand Austrian young women were working in England to learn English and escape unemployment in Austria. The Austrian Sisters of Good Tidings, of which my sister Ruth was a member, ran a hostel in Brook Green, Hammersmith, London, for the benefit of these young women. A priest looked after the psychological and spiritual well-being of these girls, and the sisters helped us in more worldly things.

On weekends, we met in the hostel to have a good time and exchange experiences. With the help of the Austrian Embassy, particularly Mrs. Breitenfels from the social department, I got work in the West London Hospital, situated in Hammersmith close to the Austrian hostel. I cleaned twenty-eight rooms every morning between seven and noon. On three afternoons and every second weekend, I had to work again between five and eight in the evening, serving dinner to the patients and to hungry medical trainees, collecting the dishes, and cleaning up the kitchen. As I worked in the private wing of the hospital due to my ability to speak Italian and some French besides German, I met only rich patients from different parts of the world. Sweetheart, you were most impressed when I told you of John Hollingsworth, a conductor of the BBC orchestra, who tested my English vocabulary every morning while I was mopping his floor, because he gave me homework every day. I had to learn the words in the "Unusual Vocabulary" section of the *Reader's Digest*. We had wonderful conversations about music and musical performances. Once he asked me which of the proms I would like to go to and handed me a program to choose five performances. I noticed that he conducted the first part of one of the performances. After the intermission it was Sir Malcolm Sargent's turn. Before Hollingsworth was discharged from the hospital, he called for me and gave me tickets to my chosen performances. Of course, I was overwhelmed and even more so, when I found myself sitting in his loge.

Every afternoon, I took the bus to the West London College of Commerce to study English language and literature, as well as English history in courses for foreign students. There I met my first Asians and Africans. Mrs. Richmond, our main teacher, guided us through Shakespeare's London, took us to tea at Selfridge's, and showed us an unexploded bomb that had hit that department store during World War II. She introduced me to a member of the BBC orchestra and gave me tickets to their dress rehearsals. At one of them, I listened to Mstislav Rostropovich playing his cello. It was awe-inspiring. I had told her of my love of classical music and my ten years of voice instruction by a Latvian concert singer. So one day she surprised me with an invitation from Gladys Palmer (*1898), an American contralto from Ohio, who had sung under Bruno Walter's baton. Mrs. Palmer gave me singing lessons during the time of my stay in London. How could I have been so lucky! I spent many evenings at Covent Garden or Saddlers Wells hearing the greatest singers of that time and marveling at their performances, or I went to the Royal Festival Theatre to enjoy concerts and ballets. Plays and visits to the British Museum and to the Tate Gallery were also on my list of enjoyment and learning. Looking back, sweetheart, I remember the times you and I had season tickets to the Festival Theatre, the Playhouse, and the Opera House in Adelaide, where we heard Joan Sutherland, Yehudi Menuhin, and many other world-famous musicians. Classical music was as much part of your life as mine and was wonderful to share.

I told you of one really bad experience at the West London Hospital. One of those rich patients wanted to see me on my knees, so she asked me every morning why I did not wash her floor on my knees. One morning I had had enough of it, leaned my mop on her bed, held it with both hands and said, "If you English women did not have the girls from the Continent to clean your dirt away, you would die in your dirt!" ... and left the room. I heard her ring her bell and disappeared into the next room. Needless to say, I had caused an uproar ... and Sister Griffith fired me. I packed my suitcases in my room in the nurses' quarters and was about to go to the Austrian hostel when an Irish orderly knocked at my door and told me that Matron ("matron knows best" was the standard expression in regard to her power in a hospital) wanted to speak to me. That sounded serious. I went there, and after a discussion where I explained my action, she reinstated me but in a different wing. I was transferred immediately to a wing for general patients, with one section of twelve beds for women and another for men. My problem there was a Pakistani who claimed to be a major in the Pakistani army and mobbed me while he was still on the ward and after his discharge from the hospital. I had to get security to get rid of him. You were quite shocked when I told you those stories.

A really good and very important experience was my encounter with an English woman who was married to an Australian sea captain. She talked to me daily at length about Australia and kindled my interest in that continent. Before she was discharged, she told me that her husband was on his way to Southampton and London. She promised to invite me to her home in Surrey after his arrival. She lived up to her word. One day I received a phone call from a Dr. Silverstone asking me to be ready at five in the evening, as we would drive to Surrey to meet the captain. There I ate my first kangaroo meat! Little did I know what was to come fifteen years later: my migration to Australia. However, as you know, long before my eventual settlement in Australia, I had spread my wings to explore the United States.

*****

Sweetheart, I have talked about my camp-counseling time in the United States already. As I had enough of the camp after seven weeks, I accepted an invitation from my Gassner relatives to spend time with them in Wisconsin. Marathon, Wausau, Superior, Phillips, Milwaukee, Sheboygan, and Madison are just some of the places where my relatives are still living. The first, Michael Gassner, had originally migrated to Montana in the mid-1800s, but soon moved to Marathon, Wisconsin. There, on the original Gassner farm, about sixty descendants of Michael had assembled to meet and welcome me to the clan. One of them, Joe, exclaimed, "Look at her; she has the same brown eyes we have! She must be a Gassner!" It was certainly bewildering to meet so many of my relatives. I was assured that there were very many more in other parts of the United States. A reporter of the local newspaper interviewed me and published an article with a photograph about my visit. These relatives came from all walks of life. They were farmers, shopkeepers, businesspeople, tradesmen, teachers, and the like. The last to arrive was Richard Gassner, the only banker in town at that time. A murmur went through the crowd when he was spotted: Richard is coming! He seemed to be the uncrowned king of the clan. I was invited to a meal and was expected to visit each family, but I only had one more week to spend before returning to New York to start the trip around my chosen part of the United States, the payment for my work in the camp. I so much enjoyed my time with my relatives that I decided to visit them more often. I did just that in the next several years and met the next generation as well. I believe most of them are university educated now, with several medical doctors and engineers among them. Some of the last three generations have visited Gassner relatives in Austria over the years, and whenever someone comes, we have a wonderful time with them. Only days before my father died in 1977, he asked Ruth to let me know that I should keep up the contact with our American relatives as he had done before me.

*****

In the spring of 1963, the state inspector of schools of Vorarlberg offered me the position of resident director at Wagner College, a Lutheran university on Staten Island. That college had a study abroad program in Bregenz, the capital city of Vorarlberg—only some fifty kilometers from Bludenz. It meant that I had to move to Bregenz and teach there at a secondary school, as well as look after up to seventy-two American college students. I was also asked to teach them education and, as part of the course, to take them to schools to observe Austrian teachers teaching English. I was thrilled to be given such an opportunity and accepted it with great enthusiasm. I believe the inspector selected me for that position because I had applied for an extended summer vacation to be able to work as a camp counselor that summer. After the trip through parts of the United States (as I told you before, sweetheart, that was my pay for seven weeks of camp work) I had to go to Wagner College, spend a week there on the campus, meet the college president and some of the staff and students, and get acquainted with American college life. It was all new to me and somewhat astonishing, because I found the students rather immature in their behavior and amazingly outspoken. I met the director of the study abroad program, Dr. Pinette, a Franco-German, and his French wife. In October I sailed with them and some fifty students on the *Hanseatic* from New York to Cherbourg. It was my first voyage across the Atlantic. It took eight days, and we were battling a hurricane. We arrived in Cherbourg about ten hours late. I had a harrowing time on board due to the fact that all of my students were Lutherans, and most of them had never drunk any alcohol and had never had so much pocket money. I had a heck of a time to keep them sober and orderly. The Pinettes were in first class, while I was in a single cabin, along with my students in tourist class. Once a day I had to report to the director about the students and their actions. In one way, I was happy about the hurricane, because many in my care got seasick—I did not—which eased my job to some degree.

As soon as we were out of the storm, the students continued partying, some of them getting stone drunk. Once we arrived in Cherbourg, two buses of the Hagspiel Company from Hittisau in Vorarlberg were waiting near the pier to take us to Paris. More than half the students traveled in my bus, most of them sleeping all the way. I felt sorry for them because they were missing out on the beautiful countryside as well as the World War II military cemetery that I saw along the road.

It was the first time in Paris for me and most of my students. Dr. Pinette, an art historian, conducted us through this amazing city, showed us many most beautiful works of art and explained their style and importance masterfully in the three days we spent there. Then the buses took us to Bregenz and the Hotel Weisses Kreuz, where we spent the next eight months.

During that time, sweetheart, we made several excursions; for instance, to Munich, Rome, Pompei, Vienna, Salzburg, Berlin, and even to Sicily, where we stayed for a whole week. It was very difficult for me to keep the students in line. In Bregenz, some of them became homesick in the beginning; later they complained about the food and the midnight curfew, which I had to control. On trips, there was always somebody who did not turn up on time for the next leg of the journey. I do not remember, my dear, if I ever told you that on another occasion, it was in 1972—I was accompanying a group of Wagner College students on a choir tour through East and West Germany—I lost a student, the only African American girl we had, and nobody noticed it, including me. I used to ask, "Has everybody got his/her neighbor?" but at that time nobody said anything. Only when I handed out the room keys in Kassel, Germany, did I notice Terry was missing. I got upset. I contacted the railway station and told them there might be a passenger without a ticket on a train, because she had left her handbag with her wallet in the bus and therefore had no money. Then I phoned the local police and the American army military police, as there was a large US base in Kassel. A few hours later, Terry arrived flanked by two US soldiers, MPs. All's well that ends well!

*****

Sweetheart, I will never forget the day in 1963 (twenty-second November), when President Kennedy was assassinated in Dallas, Texas. As it was my day off, I spent it at home in Bludenz. When I returned to the Weisses Kreuz, the students were in shock. Many of them cried. There was a fight for the hotel telephone—no cell phones in those days. Some wanted to fly home immediately, some were consoling others, and some flung their arms around me and wanted to be held. It was my time to be a mother, a counselor, a caregiver, and a psychologist. They were extremely emotional and worried that a war would break out now, the country would collapse, and the stock market would crash. They wanted to be with their families at that time of national tragedy. The Pinettes came to help me cope with that scenario. Nobody went out that night. By midnight, the waves of emotion had subsided, and everybody went to bed. I decided not to check the rooms at curfew time, the only time in my four years with the college that I did not check.

*****

I crossed the Atlantic with American students three times, and it was an ordeal every time. Once I lost four students in Versailles. We had finished our tour through the chateau and boarded the buses, when I noticed it. We waited for ten minutes, and then I told the drivers to depart. I had warned the students about my insistence on punctuality, but they obviously did not believe me. I thought word had spread on the home campus that in matters of punctuality, be it on trips or the curfew in the hotel Weisses Kreuz, I was very strict. Experience in my teaching career had taught me that I had to be strict and predictable from the beginning, not halfway through the eight months we were together. Of course, I felt somewhat uneasy having left these people in Versailles, but when I heard that a son of the chairman of the board of trustees of the college was among the missing, I was relieved, because I knew that he had already been in Paris with his parents and had done matriculation in French. We were scheduled to go to the opera that night. I had all the tickets. Lord behold, literally seconds before we boarded the buses to take us there, the four arrived, and we were complete again. I did not reprimand them, as I did not want to ruin the performance for them; I just gave them a stern look. They apologized on the way back.

*****

My last crossing with Wagner College students was on the *QE1* of Cunard Lines (*Queen Elizabeth 1*), one of the largest ships at that time (1965). It was a most challenging voyage for all on board. In the first days of the voyage, I had the usual problems with my students concerning their consumption of alcohol and, consequently, their behavior. The ship was very large, and I had seventy-two students in my care. Needless to say, sweetheart, I could not be everywhere at the same time. One day out of New York harbor, a hurricane warning was announced. Word had spread on the Wagner campus about hurricanes, as we had gone through one every other time previously. Many students were scared and huddled together and soon disappeared into their cabins. Seasickness affected me like most passengers and some of the crew. High waves hit the portholes, and the ship rocked terribly despite good stabilizers. My suitcase slid from side to side on the cabin floor. I felt most miserable, weak and nauseated. I could not possibly leave my cabin to find out how the students were faring. On the third day, a steward opened my cabin door, checked my pulse and my blood pressure, brought me a glass of water, and then dragged me onto the deck to get some fresh air. There I found some of my group and lots of other passengers. From the loudspeaker, a voice told us that we were at the tail end of a bad hurricane and would soon be out of it. The fresh air was a relief. Despite the discomfort, I found this ordeal actually quite interesting and watched the ship rolling from right to left and up and down and found it best to roll along with it. We could not stand and hold on to the ship's railing for long, as water still splashed on deck and made it slippery. Eventually we were herded into the dining room, where food was served. A frame around the tables prevented any china or cutlery from sliding off the tables. I was glad to get something to eat, even if it was not one of those wonderful meals one gets on first-class cruise ships. The next day we were invited to join groups of passengers who were interested in being shown the damage the hurricane had done to the ship. Of course, I took part along with some of my students. We were even taken to the bridge, where the captain and his first mate explained how they had steered the ship through that turmoil, and to the engine room, where one of the engines needed some repair. When I think of you, sweetheart, being on navy ships in hell and high waters, never knowing how close the enemy was, and in fear of torpedoes, I realize it literally must have been sheer hell for you. My experience on the *QE1* had given me just an inkling of what could happen on even a large ship. It turned out to have been my worst voyage ever. Our three cruises together on the P & O Lines to the South Seas and my two Atlantic crossings as a Fulbright student on the *Independence* of the American Export lines were smooth sailings compared to my three Atlantic crossings in September 1963, 1964, and 1965, the last one being the worst. We arrived in Cherbourg twenty-three hours behind schedule.

*****

As I told you a long time ago, on the twentieth of August 1966, I left Austria to go to New York as a Fulbright student to study first at Wagner College (BA), followed by studies at CUNY (Hunter College, MA, in 1969, and PhD at the Graduate Center of CUNY in 1973). The most formative years of my life were about to begin. During my first year at Wagner College, I lived on campus and did not enjoy it. Having already taught in Austria for twelve years, at primary as well as at middle schools, and having lived with American students in Wagner's study abroad program, where I had taught methodology as well as education—in other words, having been confronted with American bohemian life already—I should have known what to expect on an American campus. My room was nice, the food tolerable, and the library good, but discipline in the dormitories was sorely missing. In Bregenz, the students were not allowed to make any noise after midnight, but there on campus the students seemed "to come to life" shortly before midnight, stay out until the wee hours and return noisily every night, but particularly on weekends. The student council appeared to be ineffective. And the proctors? I never found out what they actually did. As I was and still am in the habit of going to bed by ten, I had a problem sleeping in the dorm, as I was woken up every night by the noise. Besides studying, I had to teach three courses of German every semester.

My worst problem at Wagner College was the fact that in those days nobody could get a BA without having passed a course in economics. In my formal education in Austria, there was no such subject as economics on the curriculum, either in high school or in teachers' college. All I knew about economics was that you do not spend money if you have not got it. Live within your means was the motto in my family. At Wagner College, we had a professor who had come to America from the Allgäu, southern Germany. In my class there sat a lot of my German students. As the professor entered the room and walked down the aisle, he gave us a test, on which we had to write the answers on the spot. One of the questions was "Which is bigger, AT&T or Prudential?" Another question was "What is a closed shop?" I had no idea. He gave us ten such factual, seemingly general knowledge questions, but I could not answer any of them. What a disaster! So many of my students in that class! How could I face them, if they found out that I had no inkling of something with which every student present was familiar? The professor's lecture lasted for two hours on every Wednesday afternoon during the summer semester. One of his most memorable statements was "When the chips are down, Charley looks out for Charley." I had no idea what chips were outside of potato chips. By the way, his name was Charley. But I realized that when Charley looks out for Charley, it is a self-centered attitude and therefore questionable, according to my upbringing. Well, sweetheart, today I know that economics ought to be taught in Austrian schools, for if it were, we might not have as many people living beyond their means and in poverty as we have.

At the beginning of the following economics class, the professor brought the tests back and read the results out aloud. Getting to my name—he returned the tests alphabetically—he announced, "Gassner, zero out of ten." I was frustrated, and my German students giggled. After class, I fronted up to him and explained my situation, and I apologized for not ever having studied economics in Austria. I asked him not to read out my results in front of the class again. He agreed, but when my name came up, he always noticeably stopped short, so that it was very obvious that my name was omitted. I felt terrible. For me it was the hardest subject I have ever had to study. The minute I read the first page of an assignment, I fell asleep. That way I got numerous zeros out of ten until I realized that this could not go on throughout the entire summer school course. I had to think of a way to study and retain the material. Fortunately I got a brilliant idea. Usually the dormitory was unoccupied in the early afternoons. So I took my economics book, went into the bathroom, filled the tub with cold water and sat in it to read my god-forsaken book and memorize the important parts. That whole summer, nobody disturbed me in my studies. Gradually my results improved, and by the end of the course, I managed a grade C, a pass, without which I would not have been awarded a BA, a prerequisite to be admitted to graduate school. Looking back on that course now, I am glad I was exposed to it, because it made me understand, to some degree at least, how business and the stock market work. Without it, I would probably never have invested in any blue chips in my life! Professor Charley has been in my mind ever since. Contrary to my course in economics, I had a great time studying public speaking for two semesters and achieved a distinction.

At the end of my first Fulbright year, in 1967, I was awarded a BA degree by Wagner College, the gateway to further studies. My next academic aim was an MA degree. However, that was not easy to achieve, because I needed a second Fulbright Scholarship, which is not easily granted. Normally these scholarships are awarded for one year with the understanding that the recipients return to their home country at the end of it. Before accepting the scholarship, the recipients have to sign a document to that effect in their home country. I sent an application for a second year, along with references regarding my achievements during the first year, to the Fulbright Commission and to the International Institute of Education (IIE) in New York. In turn, I was asked to speak to a meeting of scholarship sponsors about racial issues in America.

The year 1967 was the beginning of race riots in many American cities and at universities. Fortunately, I had taken those two courses in public speaking! Just as important was the fact that in 1963 I had lived for a few days in a black American middle-class family in Chicago and had grasped the opportunity to meet young people who had participated in Martin Luther King's march on Washington. My talk must have been well received, for I won a second Fulbright Scholarship. Of course, my sweetheart, I spent most of that summer with my family in Austria. After my return, I enrolled in the master's program at Hunter College of the City University of New York (CUNY) to study German philology and literature as well as linguistics. The department head gave me an assistantship to teach language courses there; after all, I had been a teacher in Austria for twelve years, and I was allowed to continue living at, and teaching German at, Wagner College on Staten Island.

*****

During that year, sweetheart, I moved out of the dormitory and in with Marie, the secretary to the dean of Wagner's Graduate School, a confirmed vegetarian spinster who had her own house, in which I occupied a bedroom and a bath but shared the kitchen with her. I cooked my regular meals while she ate mainly raw vegetables, nuts, and kernels of all sorts. She was very skinny and enjoyed watching me cook and eat. Very occasionally, she would accept an invitation to share my meal with me. She was a great philosophizer and total supporter of Ronald Reagan and Richard Nixon, while I was on the side of Robert Kennedy. During the presidential campaign of Nixon and Kennedy, we had numerous political discussions until she found out that I had become a volunteer campaign worker for Robert F. Kennedy. That changed our relationship somewhat. On the sixth of June 1968, while I was staying at a friend's apartment in Manhattan because I wanted to take an early bus to Montreal, Canada, the next morning, news came over the radio that Kennedy had been assassinated at a hotel in Los Angeles. You know, sweetheart, I burst into tears, as my students had done in Bregenz, when President Kennedy lost his life due to an assassin's bullets. I immediately called some other campaign workers and joined them in the city to lament his death. Needless to say, I did not go to Montreal, as I wanted to be near St. Patrick's Cathedral to attend the funeral service from the street. It was clear to us that we would not have a chance to get into St. Patrick's. I returned to Staten Island to find Marie most sympathetic and understanding. He was the third male Kennedy to lose his life: first Joe in World War II, then Jack, and now Robert. Little did I know that within six months, I would meet and be involved with several members of the Kennedy clan.

I told you, sweetheart, that I had heard Andy Williams sing the "Battle Hymn of the Republic" in a most moving rendition while I was standing outside St. Patrick's at RFK's funeral Mass. When you left me, I thought of a dignified way to farewell you in our church in Bludenz. RFK's funeral came to my mind, and I asked Lukas and his Turkish friend Cenk, our neighbor, to play that hymn for you, a US Navy officer, who had been ready to give his life for his country as a young man. The two boys each played it beautifully on their saxophones, Lukas in the evening at the farewell ceremony and Cenk the next morning at the Resurrection Mass. You had always so enjoyed the music they had played for you at your birthdays.

Sweetheart, prior to RFK's assassination, on the fourth of April in the same year, another tragedy had occurred in the United States: Martin Luther King was killed by an assassin in the South. I was sitting on a hill in Hamilton, the capitol of Bermuda, when I heard it on the radio. What a shock that was, less than five years after his March on Washington for jobs and freedom!

*****

One night, as I was on my way back from Manhattan to Staten Island, getting off the ferry and heading toward bus 6, a man with a machete in his hand followed me. I got scared and started to run. A taxi driver realized that I was in danger, drove up to me, opened a door of his car, pulled me in, and sped off. He drove me up Grimes Hill and home to Marie's. He warned me that it was too dangerous for a young woman to be on the street alone so late at night. It was about eleven at night when this happened. I was shaken by the experience and resolved there and then to find a place to live in Manhattan, because some of my teaching at Hunter College, as well as all of my MA and later my PhD lectures, took place in the evening. I contacted the Hunter Placement Office and asked for a live-in babysitter job. None was available; however, my name was put on a waiting list.

Two days later, the office contacted me, informing me that somebody was looking for a dog sitter. I hated dogs, because I had been bitten twice by a German shepherd in Austria. At that point, I resolved instantly that from now on I would love dogs—after all, being attacked by a man with a machete was worse than having to deal with a dog. I was given the address and phone number and told to ring that person, a Mr. Lemoyne Billings, at 318 East Fifty-First Street, Manhattan. When I rang, a gruff and most unpleasant voice answered the phone. We arranged an appointment for the following day. He, with his dog at his heels, opened the door. He had a stern look and an awful voice, and I felt uneasy. The first thing I did, unintentionally, of course, was step on one of the dog's paws. "Tolly does not like that," Mr. Billings growled. He showed me the whole house—three floors—particularly the ground floor, which would be mine, if we came to an agreement. I noticed two things: first, that there were numerous modern art pictures hanging on the walls and that the rooms were filled with early American furniture; second, that there were a great many photographs of the Kennedys everywhere on both upstairs floors. My duty would be to walk and feed the dog and keep it in my part of the house, but to send Tolly upstairs the minute my prospective landlord came home from work. For that I would get the ground floor, and all bills such as electricity, water, and telephone would be paid by him. It sounded to be exactly what I needed; in fact, it was much better to look after a dog than a baby.

Before I left, he asked me, "Is there anything you want to know?" I picked up my courage and said, "How come you have so many Kennedy photographs standing around?" I noticed a shadow moving over his face as he answered, "Because I was President Kennedy's best friend." His voice had softened at that moment, and I felt immediately sorry for him and said, "And I was a volunteer campaign worker for Robert Kennedy." His voice was harsh again as he told me to go, because he was going to interview a student from NYU (New York University) next. I left to go to dinner at my second sponsors.

Frances and Alex Godwin lived nineteen blocks up on Madison Avenue. I found out that Alex knew Mr. Billings's brother, Josh; in fact, he had been at his wedding in Tennessee years ago and met Mr. Billings there. He immediately called him to vouch for me. Mr. Billings felt disturbed, as he was in the middle of interviewing that student from NYU, and told Alex so in his unpleasant voice. Alex's comment was "He has not changed since I met him the first time, but he is actually quite a funny guy." My sponsors were very much in favor of my becoming a dog sitter there and supported me in my decision. Alex knew that Mr. Billings was unmarried and led a busy social life. I was a bit worried about moving into a bachelor's house, worried about what my parents might think as well as my colleagues at Wagner and Hunter. I was going to discuss my plan with my chairman and his wife at Wagner College at the earliest opportunity and ask for their opinion, but Mr. Billings rang me the following morning to offer me the job. I accepted and afterward spoke with my chairman's wife, Eleonore. Her comment was "People who have a dirty mind will always have a dirty mind whether you live in Marie's or in Mr. Billings's house. So do what is helping you in your career." All that happened in the autumn of 1968. At the beginning of January the following year, I moved into Mr. Billings's house.

Sweetheart, I told you a long time ago what happened when I knocked at Mr. Billings's front door. A young boy opened the door and greeted me, saying, "Ah, you must be Miss Gassner. I'm Bobby. Lem is upstairs and cannot walk, because he sprained his ankle. He'll see you when he can walk again. He wants you to feed Tolly, then walk him, and afterward send him upstairs." Then he disappeared again. I did as I was told. As we returned from the walk, Tolly dashed upstairs, and I was left to my own devices. It was all a bit bewildering to me. I settled into my downstairs flat, waiting for more jobs to do. Several hours passed until Tolly was sent downstairs again for another meal and a walk. Occasionally I heard laughter coming out of a room. In the evening, I decided to work on my master's thesis. By ten o'clock I went to bed feeling very strange. The next day, I heard Bobby leave the house and a woman walk upstairs. I walked Tolly again and noticed that someone was vacuuming upstairs and talking to Mr. Billings. A while later, the cleaning woman knocked at my door and introduced herself as Lucille, Mr. Billings's housekeeper. She was a wonderful, eighty-year-old, very black woman from Harlem who cleaned the entire house. Over time she talked to me frequently about her childhood and her parents, who had been slaves in Tennessee. I grew to love her dearly. She was full of kindness and motherly feelings toward me and her employer. She normally came twice a week, but during Mr. Billings's incapacitation, and after Bobby had left, she came daily to help him. After a few days, I got the feeling that she checked on me or observed what I was doing all day. This went on for three weeks.

One evening as I returned from Hunter, I heard Mr. Billings's voice calling me upstairs. He asked me to sit with him in the library. He obviously wanted to get to know me and inquire about my background and my plans. He mixed one Bloody Mary after another and kept me in that room long after midnight. I began feeling sorry for that lonely man who could be very funny and laugh like mad, but who on the other hand could stop a conversation abruptly and ask me to leave. I realized that if I wanted to stay in that house I had to get used to him and Tolly, or leave. Well, I told you that I spent five and a half years there taking care of Tolly and, as it turned out, of him as well. Sweetheart, you met him in 1978, when I took you along on my first study leave from Australia to America. You were very impressed with Mr. Billings, and he with you. We had dinner at the Trader Vic's at the Plaza Hotel, where he ordered plenty of drinks but only two dinners. That was one of the jokes he often made, when he was with friends. He ordered two meals and three sets of cutlery to enable him to "steal" food from his friends' plates. For him, that was always a joke that allowed him to laugh and shock his guests.

We were halfway through dinner when the waiter came and announced the arrival of Bobby Kennedy, RFK's son, at Mr. Billings's home. He dropped everything and dashed off home to let Bobby into the house. You and I finished our meals and then took a cab back to the house. For you, dear, that was very unusual behavior, but for me it was not. I knew some of his friends who hated it when he joked like that. As we entered the house, we found Bobby and his English girlfriend unpacking their suitcases. You, Mr. Billings, and Bobby spent the rest of the evening in the library, while the girl, most interested in the German poet Goethe, asked me to tell her about him and his work. The next morning, all of us had breakfast together in a diner, before you and I went to the Graduate Center of CUNY, where I had work to do. It was great to meet my former professors there and introduce you to them.

I don't think I ever told you, sweetheart, that after finishing my MA in 1969 I was invited by the university to enroll in its PhD program. In those days in Europe and in Australia, no invitations were extended to an MA graduate to join a doctoral program in the form of a PhD. I think it is not happening these days either. The PhD has been introduced in most European countries only recently in conjunction with the Bologna Programme. With that invitation, I was presented with another scholarship, the Wertheim Scholarship. It allowed me to study in the New York City Public Library with clerical assistance and a desk of my own. Continuing my studies meant, of course, that I would neither return to my family, nor go back to teaching secondary school in Vorarlberg, nor work again with Wagner College students, nor be near my aging parents. My sister Ruth had taken over the latter responsibility. However, she wanted to study theology in Graz. My father understood me; my mother wanted me at home; my sisters were disappointed, and I felt as if I was sitting between two chairs. My professors and my friends in New York wanted me to stay and continue my studies. Ultimately a solution was found for my family situation. My sister managed to get outside help so that Ruth could start her two-year course in theology.

In 1968 I had a big obstacle to overcome. As mentioned earlier, a Fulbright Scholarship is normally awarded for only one year. The recipient has to sign a document agreeing to return to his/her home country at the end of that year. However, mine had already been extended for another year. During the second year, the IIE asked some of us Fulbrighters again to help with a fund-raiser by participating in a wine-tasting event. I contacted the Austrian cultural attaché and asked him for a few bottles of Gumpoldskirchner and Rotkipfler wine. My sponsors, Frances and Alex, suggested I should buy some French baguettes and some Emmentaler cheese and offer it to the guests. None of the other promoters did that. In addition, I talked about wine-making and vineyards in Austria. In fact I knew very little about it, but I prepared myself by reading a book on the subject. Needless to say, my presentation was quite a success, but it did not give me another scholarship. I had to return to Austria and apply for a new visa.

On the twentieth of August I went to Vienna in the hope that my wish would be fulfilled. At that time, a revolution in Czechoslovakia was taking place, the Prager Frühling, under Alexander Dubcek. The American Embassy in Vienna was overwhelmed with Czech visa applicants. In the midst of this commotion, I appeared with the simple request to be allowed to finish my MA at Hunter College, and without much ado, the consulate agreed. Upon arrival in New York, the immigration official shook his head, asked a few questions, and gave me a one-year visa.

At the same time, and for years to come, a social revolution was going on in America, particularly at many universities across the country. The unrest had begun already before Martin Luther King's and RFK's assassinations, but increased after their deaths. There were revolts at many universities, including Wagner College and CUNY. The Vietnam War had gotten worse under President Johnson, and African Americans wanted more rights and more justice. Students demonstrated with sit-ins (Columbia University, Wagner College and Hunter College, etc.), four students were shot during riots at Kent State University, libraries were burned (Columbia University), at Hunter College President Wexler was locked in her office and rubbish was set was alight in the corridor leading to her office. At Wagner College I had students who, at the end of a test, wrote "A, B, C," then drew a line across the test booklet and underneath wrote "Vietnam." Students who failed became subject to the military draft and were likely to be sent to Vietnam! That created horrendous pressure on teachers, at least the way I saw it. However, we were told to remain objective.

An incident at Hunter occurred that scared me. I arrived on the campus for my morning lectures and walked up to the lifts—my lecture room was on the seventh floor—but the lifts were occupied by students and did not run. I headed toward the stairs but could not walk up, because several students were blocking the access; in fact, they stretched their legs into the air, preventing me and everybody else from climbing up the steps. I rang my chairman and asked him what I should do. His answer was "You are paid to work there, so you stay until your teaching time is over. Then you can go home." I did just that, and thereby became a witness to the problems a sociology professor created, supported by a group of students. They broke into the cafeteria, took the money from the cash register, handed out to bystanders all the sandwiches and pieces of fruit they could find, and then proceeded upstairs in the building. Later I found out that President Wexler managed to call the police before the bonfire they had lit in her corridor became dangerous. Once the police had taken over, the building was cleared and everybody was told to go home. Some time that afternoon an announcement on radio and TV informed the population that Hunter College would be closed for the remainder of that academic semester. Those were very dangerous and disturbing times. I stayed home at night, if possible, or I used a taxi to get around once it was dark—if Manhattan can be dark at all.

While I lived in Manhattan I used to go to the Metropolitan Opera and to the State Opera at Lincoln Center, to Carnegie Hall, or to plays on and off Broadway at least once a week, usually with tickets I had received from the IIE and occasionally from somebody in the Kennedy families. The IIE tickets came from sponsors who could not use them at that time. At Hunter, the staff of the German Department was informed whenever a German poet or a historian was in the city as a visiting fellow attached to one of the large private universities, mostly Columbia and NYU (New York University). I enjoyed their presentations immensely, as they usually promoted their latest works. Among those visiting fellows were Max Frisch, Friedrich Dürrenmatt, Martin Walser (introducing his latest book *Das Fliehende Pferd*), Günter Grass (with *Die Blechtrommel*), et al. They read from their works either at their respective universities of residence or at the Goethe Institute, the cultural arm of West Germany. Max Frisch impressed me more than any of the others, because he spoke on a topic that I was personally confronted with and suffered under frequently, since much of his work dealt with the biblical concept *Du sollst dir kein Bildnis machen* (thou shalt not make images of either thyself or others): Leviticus 19:4. It was, by the way, at the root of problems I had with part of my family. Remember, sweetheart, two of my sisters had entered a convent, and the third remained in what was in fact a very difficult marriage. I, on the other hand, had gone out into the kaleidoscopic world of the 1960s, pursuing my academic interests. But some of my family persisted in seeing me exactly as they had perceived me in my late teenage years and into my tweens: in command of the household as soon as I came home from wherever I had just been, determined to follow my own way, and ambitious and successful. On my thirty-fifth birthday, one sister, concerned about my "worldliness," even counseled me that I had now lived half of my life and that it was about time to direct my thoughts and actions heavenward. Fortunately, others saw me differently: maturing and growing mentally and emotionally. In any case, I continued along my own path—often regretting that part of my family could not let go of their early image of me.

During the sixties and early seventies, when student and racial unrest were the order of the day, a degree of democratization took a hold on American society, and teacher evaluations began. The drive for more student involvement in the running of universities reached Australia as well, but a few years later. At Adelaide University, the results of these evaluations were published in the students' newspaper. In 1979, I found myself described as a "US marine sergeant with a heart of gold." Over time, my sister Irene saw and recognized how life made me grow and change, particularly after I met you, my sweetheart. I have not forgotten how amused you were when you read that student assessment.

*****

Living in New York had a tremendous impact on me and my future, particularly after I had left Staten Island and begun to live in Mr. Billings's house in midtown Manhattan. As mentioned above, I made great use of the prevailing cultural life there. In addition to enjoying music and theater performances, I also went to Greenwich Village and to many museums as often as possible. I was very busy soaking up culture of any kind. I enrolled in a university course entitled Art in New York in 1966 and 1967, studying Roy Lichtenstein, Andy Warhol, et al. My father was most amazed at the distinction I achieved because at home I had not shown great interest in his antiques or in family discussions on art. Mr. Billings's house was full of modern art, such as paintings by Miró, Braque, Modigliani, Picasso, Chagall, and others. It seemed to me soon that I was not only his dog sitter but also his art watcher.

We lived on East Fifty-First Street for one year and then moved to East Eighty-Eighth Street, not far away from German Town, wall-to-wall with the Guggenheim Museum. While there I came down with diphtheria. Mr. Billings was very concerned about me and brought me Campbell soups and crackers from the supermarket on days when Lucille did not come to clean. I was banned from the university for three weeks and was told to keep my illness a secret, as my chairman was worried I might spread the disease or at least get everybody there scared of getting infected.

Sweetheart, I told you that both of Mr. Billings's houses became the target of numerous burglars. The worst case of burglary I experienced happened one Saturday afternoon on Eighty-Eighth Street. I went to the Public Library at one in the afternoon to check footnotes and to read, returning at about five. Mr. Billings had intended to spend the weekend at the Kennedy Compound on Cape Cod, and I had locked up Tolly (who, being a basenji could not bark) in my bathroom. When I came home, I heard the dog whining at the apartment door and wondered what that could mean. There were two locks at the front door to get into the house and three additional locks on the apartment door. On putting the first key into the apartment door, I found the entire lock loose in its setting. The other two locks were broken, and the door just opened. A massive burglary had taken place. I was shocked and scared and ran around to check on what was missing. Then I called all the Kennedys whose telephone numbers I had, as well as Alex, my sponsor. The first to arrive was Jean Kennedy Smith's husband, Stephen Smith, who offered me a cigarette to calm my nerves. Another person thought a drink would help me and gave me a glass of whiskey, and Alex suggested Mr. Billings should be called. He came on the Kennedy plane and promised me to make up for the losses I had suffered personally. After everybody had had a drink or two, they left, and Mr. Billings sat down to work out his insurance claim. Unfortunately, I was not covered by his insurance, as I was neither registered as an employee nor as a visitor. I had lost all my jewelry, my electric clock, my TV, and a few other things of minor value. He had lost a great many personal things and gifts of President Kennedy and Senator Robert Kennedy, both dead at that time, but to my amazement, none of the paintings or any other object of art had been stolen. When he returned a few days later from an evening with the Kennedys, he brought me two boxes full of very good Kenneth Lane costume jewelry sent to me by Jean Kennedy Smith and her sister, Pat Kennedy Lawford, as well as a TV and a travel clock from Ethel Kennedy, the late senator Robert Kennedy's wife. In order to "calm my nerves" and make me feel better, he sent me on a one-week cruise in the Caribbean. Once I had gotten the taste of the Caribbean, I repeated that experience several times more in the course of my five years in Manhattan.

Talking of burglaries, sweetheart, a much worse experience was to come. One night after I had returned from the Met and gone to bed, I was woken up by the sound of rustling paper in my bedroom. I sat up, switched on the bedside lamp, and was confronted by a young good-looking man, searching about on my dressing table. He swiftly turned around, approached me with a short knife in his hand, and whispered, "Give me your money!" I wanted to scream, but my voice froze. Instead I made a move in my bed, pulling my quilt under my chin. At that moment he came closer, holding the knife next to my face and saying again, "Give me your money!" His move closer instantly "unfroze" me, and I screamed "like hell" as Mr. Billings would say, at the top of my voice. I jumped out of my bed, and the intruder dropped his arm with the knife and fled the way he had come in, namely through the bathroom window. My very loud screaming must have woken up many neighbors, as lights went on all around. Sweetheart, you know that I have a trained voice; fifteen years of voice training in Austria and in London were of great benefit in the situation in which I found myself. I dashed into the hall and, being alone in the apartment, called the police at Precinct 19. When I mentioned where I lived, thirteen policemen arrived, all at the front door. Meanwhile, the burglar had escaped. He had taken fourteen subway tokens, which I had bought on my way home from the Met, and my attaché case with tests from my students. I believe the burglar took the case thinking that my wallet would be in it, as it was locked. As a result, my poor students had to take another test. The police asked me to identify the burglar from a collection of mug shots the next day. A police car would pick me up. I found the intruder among the first fifty photos, but the policemen tried to confuse me and made me look at hundreds of shots. I insisted that it was Angelo, a good-looking young man from Puerto Rico. He was known to the precinct as a twenty-one-year-old cat burglar who had been in jail several times already and whose address they had. I was told that I had to identify him at a lineup in the station. I should be ready the next day and would again be picked up by the police. Well, two days passed, and I was not called. So I phoned the precinct only to be told that the clever thief had given a nonexistent address to the parole officer the last time he had been released from jail; therefore he could not be found. Since he and I had faced each other at a close distance, and I was sure that he would recognize me on any street, as I would him, I was scared to go out and walk to the university or to the next bus stop. In my paranoia, I took a taxi down to uni and relied on my students to walk me back the twenty blocks it took to get home. Besides, I had to see a doctor to give me Librium for the next six weeks to go to sleep at night. This was my worst experience in Manhattan.

However, I suffered another scare once on my way back from downtown. Suddenly I was confronted by three male teenagers on the uptown sidewalk of Park Avenue. One of them held a knife at my throat, another one frisked me in search of my wallet and jewelry, and the third one was on the lookout for a police car. If one walks up or down Park Avenue, one notices the doormen standing in the entrances of all the apartment blocks on either side of the street, and the traffic moving up and down the avenue. The attack lasted only a few minutes, and then the kids disappeared empty-handed. It seemed that none of the doormen had noticed anything, but that is hard to believe. They just did not want to be involved. Civil courage was rare in the days of racial unrest in large American cities. This makes me think of three other teenagers who tried to break into a car that was parked in front of Mr. Billings's house. I told him what I had noticed and also that I was going to call the police. He did not want me to do that, saying that if I did, we would probably get problems like broken windows or a burglary later at a moment opportune for the burglars and that I would have to appear at a lineup to identify them. However, I did what I thought was right and called the police. The boys were caught and taken away, and I was interviewed about the attempted break-in. When the day came for me to appear at the lineup, I could not go, as my father had suffered a stroke, and I was on my way to Austria. These experiences made it easier for me to leave New York for Australia, although I loved the exiting and stimulating life I had had there and the wonderful cultural experiences it offers. Therefore, returning to the Big Apple with you, my sweetheart, a few years later, was a homecoming of a special kind.

*****

Burglaries were not the only factor that made it less traumatic for me to leave New York, when the time came. It had always been a struggle to gain and retain the right to stay in the United States. In 1969, during one of our Bloody Mary sessions, Mr. Billings wanted to know how long I would stay in the country. I explained my visa situation to him, and he discussed it with Senator Edward Kennedy, who then undertook his first attempt to keep me in the country. In order to speed procedures up, he decided to initiate an act of Congress for me. But then the accident at Chappaquiddick intervened: Mary Jo Kopechne lost her life on the eighteenth of July 1969, as she was sitting in Senator Kennedy's car when he drove off a bridge, and the car plunged into the water. At the subsequent inquest, he was found to be innocent; however, he had lost credibility in Congress, and the planned act of Congress was prepared but never presented. From then on, I considered myself to be a casualty of Chappaquiddick (collateral damage, in today's terms).

However, by the time my visa would normally have expired, I was already engaged in a PhD program at the Graduate Center of CUNY (City University of New York). Senator Kennedy attempted to solve my visa difficulties by obtaining a green card for me. My problem was aggravated by President Nixon, who in any case wanted foreign academics to leave the United States in order to open up the American academic job market to US citizens. Senator Kennedy organized for me to meet Mr. Paul A. Cook, the director of the Facilitative Services Staff at the Bureau of Educational and Cultural Affairs at the US State Department in Washington. I had to present myself there, where I was photographed and fingerprinted and accompanied at every step in that building by an officer, probably from the FBI. Once in Mr. Cook's office I had to tell him why the United States should waive the rule requiring my return to Austria once my visa as a PhD student had expired. "Tell me—what makes you so important for this country that I should keep you here?" was his first question, followed by, "What can you contribute to American education?" At first I was stunned, but then my brain began to race. I do not remember exactly what I answered him, but the expression "to blow your own horn," which I had abhorred until that moment, suddenly took on the meaning of self-defense, of survival. After a good half hour, he took his feet off his desk, grinned, and said,

"Okay, you won." One of Senator Kennedy's secretaries, Susan Riley, had been waiting for me and took me to her office, from which I could ring Professor Anton Porhansl in Vienna, the director of the Austrian branch of the Fulbright program. His answer to my story was "Well, if Senator Kennedy wants you to stay, and Mr. Cook allows it, I can certainly not go against them. You are released." My joy was enormous, and Mr. Billings, who had wanted me to continue to be Tolly's sitter, was happy. Before I left the United States to migrate to Australia, all the documents that I had sent to the Immigration Department were sent back to me, among them all the wonderful recommendations my superiors at CUNY and at Wagner College had written on request of the Immigration Office. Reading them showed me that "blowing my own horn" in Mr. Cook's office was justified.

As US universities could only employ Americans, even after having finished my PhD I had no chance of being given an academic position at a university, as would have been necessary for permanent residency. Therefore I consider myself also a casualty of Nixon's ruling. In order to strengthen my application for permanent residency, in 1973, after having attained a PhD in Germanic languages and literatures, I accepted a job as a bilingual secretary, first in a foreign language bookshop (a job I disliked) and next in the Kennedy offices (thirty-second floor, PANAM Building.—a job I also disliked). However, likes and dislikes aside, this work finally enabled me to acquire the coveted green card in May 1974. Now, with a green card in hand, my former chairman, Professor Nordmeyer, obtained permission for me to direct and also teach in his department's summer school program from June to August 1974. Afterward, my future would again be in limbo unless I could find employment. Although I was initially offered a teaching position at the University of South Dakota, the dream fell through when I was notified that the government insisted on the employment of an American citizen that had returned from military service in Vietnam. Looking back on it, I think I was destined not to get that position, because I was meant to settle in Australia and meet you, my sweetheart.

In the meantime, the summer of 1974 found me once more living in Mr. Billings's house looking after Tolly. The end of my story with Mr. Billings came when I left him for good to accept a position at Adelaide University. His first letter to me began, "Dear Sigrid, Having known each other for about seven years it is time to drop formalities and call each other by our first names …" As mentioned previously, you, my sweetheart, wanted to meet him. So when we went to America in 1978, we stayed in his house. Less than two years later, I wrote to him, "Dear Lem, … my husband had brain surgery and will never recover … I will look after him until his end … I wonder, who will look after you some day, when you are very ill." His answer, "Dear Sigrid, … he is very lucky to have you. I do not intend to be sick long …" Soon after that, in 1981, he was found dead in his bed by a close friend. Years of emphysema and a heart attack had taken his life. I cried when my former sponsor, Alex, rang me with the sad news, for Lem Billings was a good man.

*****

A few years ago, journalist and former presidential speech writer David Pitts spent more than seven hours interviewing me by telephone from Washington to complete his historical study, *Jack and Lem: The Untold Story of an Extraordinary Friendship*. In this book, he quotes me saying, "It was a very unusual friendship. It was love, and not all love needs to be consummated." And later: "So many people comment on the fun person in him [Lem], and on so many photos he laughs. However, I am convinced that deep inside he was a sad and lonely person, in a sense a tragic antihero who didn't get what he wanted most—a life with and around JFK ..." (David Pitts, *Jack and Lem*. Carroll & Graf, NY, 2007: 304).

*****

My sweetheart, I told you so much of what Lem and I had discussed during our Bloody Mary sessions in his library that your interest in him was understandable. Lem's personality, his generosity in sharing his life's stories and his connections had influenced me and the course of my life a great deal by opening up a world for me that I would never have known existed. My more than five years in his house contributed to a large degree to making me the person I had become when you and I met in Australia.

During my years in Lem's house, I had the opportunity to meet some very famous people. Among them was the governor of Wisconsin, Patrick Lucey, with whom I discussed the amalgamation of his state's universities. My university, CUNY, consisted of five large campuses with a total student population of 196,000. Big is beautiful seems to have been in mode at that time. Governor Lucey was planning to join the two large institutions: the University of Wisconsin and the State University. He invited me to his inauguration as governor of Wisconsin, which took place on the fourth of January 1971 in Madison. As I was unable to accept his invitation, he asked me to spend some time with him and his family later that month. While I was there, he organized a guided tour through the university for me. The guest bedroom where I slept had a large bed with a ceiling and curtains made of brocade on either side, and it contained early American furniture. I had a most interesting time with the Luceys, a down-to-earth and unpretentious family. I found out that the governor had been a foundling, and his wife was Greek.

Other interesting guests at Lem's house were Jack Paar, a television celebrity, and his wife; the movie diva Lauren Bacall, who was still very sad about her husband Humphrey Bogart's death; and Andy Williams, who had sung at RFK's funeral in St. Patrick's Cathedral. Sweetheart, I told you once of Lem's party, where ten members of the international choir Up with People sang. As Lem wanted me to join the party with a male friend, I invited Jim, a fellow student who was a retired policeman—New York City police officers could retire at the age of forty, or after twenty years of service in those days because of the dangers of their job. The party was held in honor of Patricia Kennedy Lawford. I had placed Tolly in my bedroom during my presence at the party. Somehow a guest seemed to have lost his way in search of a toilet and opened my bedroom door—Tolly dashed out and ran into the middle of the party. At that moment, Pat, sitting on a low white leather couch, bent her head to the floor to pick up her glass of wine; Tolly got a hold of her hair … it was a wig! The dog raced upstairs with it, and Pat screamed and left the party in a fury.

At the front door stood two Secret Service men to observe the entrance. It was about midnight when Jim, the policeman, suddenly whispered to me that one of the Secret Service men had told him that Senator Edward Kennedy was approaching in a limousine. I swiftly informed the host. He awaited the senator at the spiral staircase that led to the party room. As soon as he arrived at the top of the steps, Mr. Billings announced, "Ladies and gentlemen, please rise; Senator Kennedy has arrived to join the party." To me it appeared as if a king had arrived. Everybody but the senator's wife, Joan, stood up. The host spoke a toast; the senator answered it, had a sip of white wine, and asked his wife to go home with him. He spent no more than about fifteen minutes at that party. Lauren Bacall was the last guest to leave. Mr. Billings and I had a Blood Mary and a good talk about the party in the library before retiring. In the morning Lucile came to clean up.

*****

Sweetheart, let this be the end of my recollections of my most fascinating years in London and in the United States. In October 1973 I sailed back to Europe with a new group of Wagner College students, only to return by plane once more to Mr. Billings and my summer school directorship at Hunter College in June 1974. The months in between, I spent as resident director of Wagner College students in Bregenz, while at the same time teaching English and German in the gymnasium in Dornbirn, some ten kilometers from Bregenz. I realized that it would be impossible for me to continue with my two positions. Therefore I prepared myself to spread my wings further and continue my life in Australia, where I was destined to meet you, my darling.

*****

On the twentieth of August 1974, I boarded the *Marconi* of Lloyd Triestino in Genoa to sail to Australia. The name *Lloyd* entered my life for the first time. I disembarked in Melbourne and took a plane back to Adelaide, as Adelaide was no longer a port of call for that shipping company. During the long voyage (arrival on the twenty-sixth of September) I had a great time. We had only two hours of rain during the entire voyage and docked at numerous ports for usually a good half day or more. At ports such as Naples, Messina, Malta, Gibraltar, and Tenerife, the number of passengers increased markedly as the ship took on migrants from different countries. Once out of the Mediterranean, the captain announced that English lessons were scheduled for all migrants to attend. As the university had sent me a first-class ticket, I was not considered a migrant. On board I met Harry, a Tasmanian sheep farmer with twenty thousand sheep, and a representative to the UN. He accompanied me to all the evening entertainments and to the bar for a daily predinner drink. He introduced me to Australian English, which is quite different from American English, as far as some words and the pronunciation of some sounds are concerned. In first class there were mostly businesspeople and Australian pensioners, who wanted to decrease their savings prior to applying for their pensions, because in those days, as I later found out, if one held more that A\$ 40,000 in a savings account, one's pension was decreased. A variety of entertainments was organized for us in first class alone. In one of the sing-along sessions, somebody alerted an officer to the fact that I could sing well. The captain sent me a letter asking me to perform one evening for the first-class passengers. I practiced with the ship's band and sang the "Barcarole" and "Wien, Wien, nur du allein," accompanied by the ship's band. The following morning, an officer brought me a card from the captain, thanking me for the performance and asking me to sing for the migrants in tourist class. After my second song, six Austrians ran on stage crying and embracing me. Homesickness before we had even arrived in Australia! The captain was worried about security and ordered an officer to guide me out of the theater. Sweetheart, I remember how proud you were when I showed you my picture in the ship's daily bulletin.

When the *Marconi* docked at Fremantle, the first Australian port, Harry and I took a taxi to Perth, where he looked for a pub, because he wanted a beer. Hm, no alcohol before eleven in the morning! How British! Alcohol from eleven in the morning till two in the afternoon, then not again until five. Pubs closed for the night at ten. Amazing! He showed me the city, and I was surprised to see so many beautiful parks in and around the city. I marveled at the unusual plants and birds and the slow pace of the people walking on the streets. Everything seemed to me in some ways familiar—somewhat British—and strange at the same time. As it was spring in Australia; the flowers and trees looked fresh and colorful, and the scent of the parks was unusual, but pleasant. The birds, mostly parrots and magpies, sounded harsh, compared to the lovely singing and whistling of birds in Europe. Only the flies were uncomfortable. We boarded the *Marconi* again toward the evening to continue our voyage nonstop along the Great Australian Bight to Melbourne. From there, I had to take a plane back to Adelaide. With Harry's help, the transfer caused me no problems. During those last few days onboard, Harry explained Australian life and culture to me and told me a lot about the Aborigines, the indigenous people of Australia. It all sounded so interesting and welcoming that I could hardly wait to get to Adelaide to meet my colleagues and start making friends. When I told the Pinettes at Wagner College in Bregenz that I was going to migrate to Australia, Mme. Pinette was most surprised and alerted me to the possibility that wallabies and kangaroos would be walking down the streets, and the most poisonous snakes were known to slither into houses and beds. Of course, I did not believe it, but when I sat in my chairman's car—Professor Brian Coghlan, his wife Sybil, and two of their four sons met me at the Adelaide airport—I did look out of the windows somewhat wondering whether it was true what Mme. Pinette had said about wallabies and kangaroos. Well, all I noticed to be strange were the numerous young Aussi men who had beards. I wondered why that was, as it was supposed to get to forty-two degrees Celsius in summer.

The university had booked a flat for me, where I could stay for three weeks free of charge. The Coghlans helped me with my luggage and then left me with the promise to come and take me to their house for dinner and to meet the deputy head of the department. About two hours later, the head of my department, Brian Coghlan, knocked at my front door and entered with a bottle of Claret, his favorite Australian red wine, under his arm. He opened the bottle and, in true Aussi style, welcomed me to Australia. After about two hours, I knew what was important for me to know before entering the seventh floor of the Napier Building and meeting the staff and secretary of the German Department, later called the Department of European Studies, which then included French, English, and linguistics as well as German. In the course of the democratization at the university, the department heads became elected chairpersons, a change which Brian considered to be a demotion. Chairpersons are to be elected by the departmental staff. Back to my welcoming dinner! Sybil had prepared a stew, potatoes, and a salad, followed by a dessert, which one had to have, as Brian was an Englishman who needed his "pudd" at the end of every meal. The deputy head, Tony Stephens, an Australian, was among other things a Rainer Maria Rilke specialist and always soft-spoken. Brian's interests lay in a variety of authors (e.g., Theodor Storm, Hugo von Hofmannsthal, and particularly Richard Wagner and his *Musiktheater*). Brian was a man of large gestures and with a deep, sonorous voice, both of which he used most effectively.

The dinner conversation dealt mostly with departmental matters. I was told that my major responsibilities were language teaching and program direction at all levels—the department did not have a linguist then—as well as meeting all high school students throughout the entire state of South Australia who were planning to matriculate in German. As part of my job I traveled yearly, sometimes by airplane, to all the high schools where German was taught. For the next five academic years I, as chief examiner of the state's Public Examination Board, had to supervise the matriculation of all German language students with the help of a panel of German teachers, selected by me. In the department, I had to give six language classes per week, make myself available to the students at three set hours weekly, and in addition be available to them by appointment. We had frequent staff meetings and, of course, I, being the new "bloke" on the staff, was given the job of secretary at such meetings in the first two years. University committee work was also handed out to us. As the only linguistic specialist, I had the departmental representation to the language laboratory as a further obligation. The rest of the time was to be spent on course development, preparation, and publications. Meals were taken in the staff club or in the student union. I remember well how Lloyd enjoyed a lunch there, when the weather was too bad to sit in the grass at the river Torrens, where we watched little boats and the *Popeye* floating by. Our lunches together were always a special treat in fostering our relationship as a couple.

Our first staff meeting ended, like many subsequent staff meetings, with a luncheon in the city, usually in the suburb called Norwood. Claret flowed freely—no wonder, as South Australia is a world-famous wine-growing area, and Australians generally seem to like a glass or two with lunch—and luncheons took up quite a bit of time. On one such occasion, I ate myself almost sick on shrimp, with the result that I came to work the next morning with a terrific stomachache. My colleagues sent me to the staff-and-student doctor, who gave me an injection of morphine and a referral to an x-ray clinic for an x-ray scheduled for the next day. He ordered a colleague to drive me back to my apartment. The colleague kindly stayed until I had woken up from the shot, and I could assure him that I was all right. The next morning I had my x-ray, which showed a medium-sized hernia. Obviously a piece of my stomach had gotten stuck in it, causing me to feel so sick. From then on I made sure never to overeat again, particularly not on seafood, however delicious it might be.

My first Christmas Eve I spent with the Coghlan family, although some family members were unwell. Brian, the Englishman from Birmingham, had studied in Austria for four years, and Sybil, being Jewish and having lost all her close family members in concentration camps, had grown up in England. Family life reflected the British connection in every aspect of their lives, including Christmas pudding and cricket during the Christmas holidays (which are the academic year's main holidays). What present should I bring, my biggest worry at that time! I decided to bake my mum's favorite Christmas cookies using many shapes and forms. The four Coghlan boys enjoyed them very much for the next few Christmases—until the boys outgrew them. As they liked my ducks best, they called them "Dr. Gassner's duckies" and later "Dr. Sigi's duckies."

That first Christmas in Australia was cold and rainy, therefore quite a disappointment; after all, I had read that Christmas is celebrated mostly on the beaches. By that time I had already met a number of German teachers because the German Language Teachers Association of South Australia had held a conference shortly after my arrival—among other things, to welcome my arrival. Many of the teachers invited me into their homes and schools, so that I did not feel lonely at any time. Of course, there were my colleagues from the university who were also most generous in giving me their time to make me feel welcome. After Christmas, I spent a week in the Adelaide Hospital to undergo minor surgery. As I had made friends with some elderly couples from Sydney and Melbourne, among them a man in his eighties from Melbourne for whom I had arranged a birthday party on board the *Marconi*, I had to write some Christmas cards. Upon reading of my hospitalization, the Heggies from Melbourne invited me to spend the first two weeks after discharge from the hospital with them. Oh, I so enjoyed the early cup of tea at six in the morning that Edna brought to my bedside! Breakfast I took with her after eight in the morning. One day, when Edna had an appointment, and I was alone in the house, I studied the city's new telephone directory in search of Hans Föger, a cousin who had migrated to Melbourne in 1960. Before I left Austria in 1974, I had to promise my father to find him, the son of his sister. After several tries I found a name I thought could be his under John K. Foeger. I decided to write him a letter and let him decide whether he wanted to be found or not, as he had never written to my father, his uncle. I invited him to call me in three days between four and six in the evening, if he wanted contact. Hans rang me at the first opportunity and immediately jumped into his car with his son Raimund to meet me. He lived in a suburb thirty kilometers out of Melbourne. He took me to his house, and we rang my father in the evening, it being morning of the same day in Bludenz. Ruth, who was at home with him, told me later that Dad was crying for some time, crying out of happiness that Hans had been found. Four years later, Hans and Raimund visited their relatives in Bludenz for the first time since 1960. During my twenty-four years in Australia, we visited each other many times.

Within days after my first appearance in the university, I found a message on my desk one morning from a Peter Steidl, Commerce Department. I contacted that person only to find out that he was from Vienna and that he and his wife wanted to welcome me to Adelaide. We lunched together in the staff club on the following day and afterward drove to their flat in one of the suburbs. Adelaide was most awkward to get around in because of the city's bus system. All buses started in the center of the city and returned there again. So if you wanted to go from one suburb to another, you had to go into the city first and there change buses in order to get out in a different direction. It was most time-consuming. About ten years later, a circle line was established that eased the situation for some areas. It did not help me, living in Glenunga. As I could not drive, I relied on buses to get to the city center, where the university is situated. So, whoever invited me felt he/she had to pick me up and drive me home later. That was sheer Australian courtesy. Nobody expected you to take a taxi to or fro. My social life became much easier when my sweetheart entered my life, as he had a company car.

Peter Steidl took me in his car to the Austrian Club until Lloyd became my driver. There I met many compatriots, coming mostly from Carinthia, Styria, Upper Austria, and Vienna. These people wanted to escape unemployment at home in the '50s and '60s. There we ate authentic home-cooked Austrian food every Friday night, ate and danced every second Saturday night, and celebrated Austrian National Day on the third Sunday in October. On dancing nights the Schuhplattler was usually performed by young second-generation Austrian boys, and the girls showed the dirndls their parents had brought from Austria. These were always wonderful times. One heard a variety of Austrian dialects, but rarely the dialect of Vorarlberg. Occasionally the Choir of the Austrian Club of Melbourne came to visit and sang Austrian songs. Once the F1 driver Gerhard Berger and my nephew Martin Reiter, secretary of the Austrian Tennis Association and organizer of the Davis Cup then, visited our club. Many of our people seemed to have spells of homesickness, probably just like some people in all the other clubs of European migrants. The German Club was many times larger than the Austrian Club, the Swiss Club rather small. The Italians and Greeks had several clubs—after all they made up the largest number of migrants.

At the first Austrian National Day shortly after my arrival, Peter gave "the talk," but disliked doing it. So from then on it was my duty to alert our people to our "big day." Although Lloyd did not understand a word I was saying when I held my speech, he was proud of me delivering this service to my home country. The hall was always decorated with plenty of Austrian flags, the national anthem was sung, the Schuhplattler performed, and afterward coffee and delicious homemade cakes were served. Whoever had a dirndl wore it, and many men wore Styrian or Tyrolian suits. We always had a festive and joyful time.

A year later, Lloyd and I and some friends celebrated Christmas together. Right afterward, we tried out our newest acquisition, a car camper, and traveled for three weeks along the eastern coast of Australia, stopping at several places along the Great Ocean Road, singing in the car and enjoying each other's company. Several times we stayed up quite late and watched nocturnal animals at their activities. We camped quite often in forest areas near a river or at the seaside, cooking our meals and having frequent barbecues. Lloyd had come to live in Australia after his honorable discharge from the US Navy (Korean War). Prior to the Korean War, he had served in the Pacific War. When the marines were given short service leave, they were always sent to Australia. So he was quite familiar with the Australian wildlife and countryside, while for me it was a wonderful revelation of nature. The smell of the sea, the fragrances in the woods, the sounds of parrots in the morning and at night, the sight of sleeping koalas, jumping kangaroos and wallabies, and running emus—all of it was new to me. I was only scared when we were told by another camper on the Jindabyne campgrounds that a red-back spider had crawled into our car camper, and, later on, a brown snake had been spotted near us by someone. These two creatures being most poisonous put a bit of a damper on my enthusiasm for camping. In the Snowy Mountains, we visited the big dam and were told that Austrian engineers had had a hand in building it.

One morning we decided to "climb" Mount Kosciuszko (about twenty-three hundred meters). What a joke that was! A bus took us to the highest post box of Australia. From there it was a short jaunt to the top of the mountain. Lloyd surprised everybody in our group and especially me, when suddenly he spread his arms wide and yelled at the top of his voice and for all Australia to hear, "I love Sigrid!" I was embarrassed and threw a snowball at him. By the way, that was the only time I saw any snow in Australia. No wonder the mountain range is called Snowy Mountains! On the way back, we stopped at Threadbo and noticed that several houses for tourists had Austrian names such as Arlberg and Tyrol, just like in Mammoth Lakes (Sierra Nevada, California), where Lloyd's brother Jared lived. We entered a souvenir shop there to find the same Austrian souvenirs that tourists can buy in my hometown Bludenz. We were told that many skiing instructors in the Snowy Mountains come from Austria and work here in the Australian winter which, of course, is the Austrian summer. We left the Snowy Mountains in time to spend New Year's Eve at Whiskey Bay feasting on roasted chicken, drinking some "bubbly" (Australian champagne), and enjoying the sight and sound of ocean waves coming in and going out again in their own rhythm. No music, no noise, no firecrackers, just silence but for the waves. What will the new year have in store for us? Getting married? Yes! Our engagement was nearing the end of its third month. Our honeymoon in Austria, meeting my family, introducing my sweetheart to my extended family and to friends and neighbors? How will they receive him? He does not know enough German to speak with them. Another course in the university's Continuing Education School will probably do him good. These were some of the ideas we discussed there on the beach at the beginning of the new year.

On looking back, I have to say that we could realize our plans and that all went very well.

*****

Getting married on the twenty-ninth of November of that year was not easy for me. How would I cope with this new situation after so many years of "freedom"—after all, I was already forty-two years old?

My cousin Hans and Lloyd's friend and sports coach Gyula Czesko were our witnesses to the event and Rev. Craig was our clergyman. The meal took place in the staff club of the university with fifty-eight guests. A minor but for me amazing aspect was that as far as Lloyd's sales team was concerned, during cocktails the men, all of them British or Aussies, stood on one side of the room near the bar, their spouses sat opposite in a row along the wall. The rest of our guests were mostly migrants and colleagues from my university, who mixed and moved around.

During the first year after our wedding, I left Lloyd for a few weeks to travel to Dresden in the German Democratic Republic as a delegate to an International Conference of German Teachers. It was my first stay in a communist country. He was amazed at all the stories I could tell him after my return. We had to stay in a large towerlike building that during the year housed university students. On my floor were delegates from several countries, including many from the Soviet Union. Besides attending or speaking at lectures and taking part in seminars on anything that had to do with the teaching of the German language and German culture, we were shown the city, went to a very good concert and visited parts of the Zwinger (museum). I found it interesting to see many beautifully restored buildings with a metal board fastened to the front wall informing the viewer that the building had been destroyed during World War II by the Allies and rebuilt by GDR craftsmen. At the end of the conference, we were taken on a bus tour to Meissen (porcelain factory), Eisenach (J. S. Bach), Wittenberg (Martin Luther), Weimar (Goethe and Schiller), and other historically and culturally most interesting places. Nobody was allowed to travel independently by order of the East German police. While still in Dresden, I noticed that I was about to lose the heel on one of my shoes. A conference guide directed me to a shop where six shoemakers were sitting in a line to repair shoes. People queued up to get to the table where women accepted your shoes, checked them, and in my case, told me off: Why had I not brought the shoe in earlier, because now it needed more nails than it would have, had I come sooner and had I been more careful. Before I could answer, she detected my conference label and reproached me for having waited in line, when I could have jumped the queue as a guest of the GDR. My shoe was repaired immediately and returned to me with the comment that I should have bought shoes in the GDR, where I would have found better quality. Needless to say, I was glad to get out of this place and glad that Lloyd was not with me!

In 1977 I left him alone again for several days, because I was invited to represent Adelaide University at an international conference in Dunedin, New Zealand, held in honor of the Austrian poet Franz Grillparzer and arranged by an Austrian professor who chaired the German Department at the university of that city. The guest of honor was Professor Weiss from the University of Salzburg. I was amazed at how many lecturers from various parts of the world had assembled in Dunedin (South Island) to discuss Grillparzer's work at that most southern university of the world. Lloyd had told me about his temporary stay on the North Island in 1943, while in the Pacific theater during World War II, and made me curious to set foot in that country. After the conference, I had time for an enjoyable bus trip on the North Island. I found the New Zealand of that time about fifty years behind Australia in its lifestyle: slower, more relaxed, and more typically English. Of course, the landscapes of those two islands, as different as they are, cannot be compared to the continent of Australia.

*****

As mentioned earlier, in 1978—Lloyd was still in good health—the university granted me my first study leave from May to August to study and work overseas. Lloyd joined me in my travels to the United States, Iceland, and Germany. The first highlight was our visit to the US Defense Foreign Languages Center, which is located at the Presidio of Monterey in California. I had met a member of that institute at an international conference in Colorado, United States, who invited me to observe the methodology of individual progression at work. At first we were briefed about the selection of languages to be taught and the aims of the courses. The selection was made according to the prevailing political importance of the respective countries during the Cold War. The students, of course, all being from different parts of the military, worked at their own pace and connected with their teacher as soon as they had finished a given task. This method of learning impressed me quite a bit. There were four levels of classes from beginners to native speaker levels. The top group in German, for instance, learned not only high German but also a German dialect. They had to familiarize themselves with the outlay of German cities—I saw the reliefs of Munich and other German cities—and learn German habits. We met most of the German teachers and had lunch and discussions with them at Fishermen's Warf. Each language had a floor where only the language taught was spoken at certain times. Songs and games of the various countries were taught as well. The students were certainly immersed in their subject. At the end of our visit, I had to write an appraisal of my impressions. To my surprise, I was asked if I wanted to teach there. I declined—I just could not imagine myself teaching and writing course materials in a military institution for thirty-two hours a week and only having two weeks of annual holiday. However, it was certainly worthwhile to have seen individual progression and immersion at work and carried out at its best.

After leaving Monterey, we visited a number of other universities with language departments in several states across the United States. Most students who studied German language, culture, and literature intended to teach German in American high schools. As a result of my observations, I decided to introduce a semester of specific language methodology in the German Department at my university for those students who ultimately wanted to teach German after they had finished their studies in the Education Department.

Our next stop under my study leave program was Iceland. There I studied Icelandic folklore in the folklore museum, and visited the open air museum and the art museum of Reykjavik, where I gained firsthand information on the Icelandic culture and civilization from its beginnings. In the university library, I was allowed to study the original Old Norse manuscripts. They were kept in a vaulted room. Before touching them, Mr. H. Ö. Erikson asked me to put on white gloves. Having spent study time there enabled me to enrich my lecture course on the history of the German language.

German culture and civilization was my next focus. Lloyd had to return to his work in Australia, while I spent the next five weeks in various places of West Germany. Part of that time I was the guest of the German Federal Republic. I participated along with about thirty-five other international university professors and lecturers in a three-week seminar on "German culture and civilisation since 1945," held in the Goethe Institute in Munich. At the end of it was a one-week trip to East Berlin. There we also visited Potsdam, where in the Cecilienhof the Potsdam Conference had been opened by Churchill, Stalin, and Truman. At the end, the Potsdam Agreement was signed by Attlee, Stalin, and Truman.

My last center of study was the University of Salzburg, where I had enrolled in the famous Salzburger Hochschulwochen with the philosophical topics "Values, Rights, Norms." I was particularly interested in a seminar on international law held by Professor Kimminich from the University of Regensburg. As the famous Salzburger Festival took place at the same time, I wanted to buy a ticket for my German-Australian friend Trudi, whom I had met in Salzburg, and myself to see *Jedermann*, which was performed in front of the Salzburger Dome. However, the performance was sold out. So we went into the adjoining university to find somebody to let us watch the play from a window. I showed the person my university ID card and obtained permission to watch the performance comfortably from a window directly opposite the stage. We sat on chairs and had the best view from the second floor, looking over the stage and the audience and hearing every word as clearly as could be. It was an unforgettable experience. After my return to Adelaide, I had to give a full and detailed report on my activities. The purpose of a study leave was for faculty members to study and inform themselves about developments abroad and to establish connections with universities overseas. Therefore the home university contributed substantially to the cost of any study leave.

*****

When I returned from my first study leave, Lloyd surprised me with a basenji, a middle-sized barkless dog similar to a young wild Australian dog, a dingo. We called him Tolly, remembering Mr. Billings's dog by the same name. These dogs are known to be highly intelligent, very protective and stubborn, and a total loss on streets with traffic. One day he ran into our bedroom, a strict no-no for him. Lloyd called him, but he hid under our bed and would not emerge. Lloyd stretched out his arm to grab Tolly by his collar, but the dog snapped at his hand. He could not have done anything worse, for Lloyd thought that he was the boss, and Tolly had to obey. Lloyd came downstairs and yelled, "This is a bad dog; he has to go!" I did not want this to happen. So I defended Tolly, which made the situation worse. Years earlier, Lloyd had trained several German shepherds and Labradors for the Blind Dog Association in Wisconsin and was not going to be beaten by a basenji! He wanted to take Tolly to our vet to have him put to sleep, while I, being a teacher and believing in pedagogy and training, tried to work out how we could teach him not to hide in a forbidden area again. I saw Lloyd for the first time as a person whose world could also be either black or white, yes or no, without any shades in between, without any possibility of compromise, depending on the situation in which he found himself. I begged him to give Tolly another chance until the next day, hoping that he would have calmed down by then. In the morning, contrary to his usual habit, he took no notice of the dog. Before we left for the city, I locked him as usual into the bathroom. We avoided the topic of Tolly while we were in the car. As soon as I was in my office, I called up the animal house of our veterinary school and talked to the master there. He asked me how we handled Tolly, and I found out that we knew practically nothing about basenjis, their character and their behavior patterns. These dogs come from Africa, are hunting dogs, and recognize only one master. After an hour-long discussion and advice on how to treat him and "educate" him with the help of a light and long aluminum chain around his neck, we ended our conversation. In the evening as Lloyd entered our living room, I invited him to one of our couch sessions, the first and only one in our lives initiated by me. I still kept Tolly in the bathroom so as not to raise my husband's anger and reminded him of the incident the previous day. Then I told him about my discussion with the master of the animal house and asked him if he wanted to be Tolly's master; whereas, I would basically just feed him and talk to him. That offer rekindled Lloyd's interest in dog training, and he agreed to give it a try that same evening. Tolly's life was spared because within six weeks we had a wonderful dog, having followed the master's advice without compromise. Unfortunately, Tolly died in 1980, when he wanted to cross a highway, while Lloyd was in hospital in Vienna, and the dog was in a friend's care.

In September of that year, Austrian Club member Tony Taurer and I attended a meeting at the SBS (Special Broadcasting Services) hall to establish Radio Austria. A committee was formed, consisting of Gerry Simonitsch†; Tony and his wife, Trudy†; Herbie Reiter; Heinz Fuchs; Ernst Wendler†; myself and Lloyd, who wrote our constitution. Peter Steidl presided over the election of members to the committee. Gerry was elected the first president without a specific work assignment; the others volunteered for broadcasting jobs. Through my connections to the Austrian Embassy in Canberra, I took on the duty to obtain and read current Austrian news, selecting what I thought was important for the listeners to hear. Trudy was in charge of music to be played and Herbie decided to be the disk jockey. Initially we were given half an hour a week to broadcast; later another half hour was granted to us to broadcast for the young Austrians in Australia, who wanted to hear what young Austrians listened to back home—not what we somewhat homesick oldies wanted to hear. For a while we accepted birthday and get-well wishes and played the requested music, if we had it. On one of my yearly visits to Austria, I called on the Austrian Radio Station in Vienna, told them of our program and received several LPs to take back to Adelaide. Once I collected enough money for Herbie and his wife to spend four weeks in Austria to increase his knowledge and practice of Schuhplattler at the place from which it had come. The club benefited a great deal from Herbie's effort to learn more about it. Using SBS Radio Austria in 1978, I told the story of "Silent Night" to our listeners and ended my presentation by playing an LP with the original version of that world-famous song. I was very sorry to end our involvement with Radio Austria when Lloyd had his stroke. At the thirty-fifth anniversary of our radio broadcasts in April 2013—I was visiting Adelaide at that time and participated in the celebrations—I was told that the constitution Lloyd had written is still valid.

We made many friends in our club who proved their friendship, particularly after Lloyd had fallen so ill in 1980. The club members accepted my husband as before, despite his loss of memory and the unpredictability of his behavior. I will never forget Hans Borowy knocking at our front door and asking me if I needed any help with anything, be it filling the deep freezer with meat from a farmer or finding a more suitable place to live or painting the rooms in our house. I was glad I could return his generosity when he asked us to visit his mother in Vienna a few years later and when he asked me to accompany him on his last journey: visiting him daily in his hospital room during my lunch break, calming him with my soothing words, taking away from him some of the fears of his approaching death, and getting a German-speaking priest for him, as he was about to leave this world. He died of asbestos cancer in the Royal Adelaide Hospital. His death was in fact caused by his work as a shipbuilder. I remember an insurance agent questioning his fellow club members, some of his former workmates, and me about his smoking habits: the amount he had smoked would play a decisive role in the amount of money his widow would receive from the insurance.

In 1979, we spent our recreational leave in America and in Austria. Our first stop was Hawaii, where we visited the memorial site of the *Arizona*, one of the ships that was sunk by the Japanese in the Pacific during World War II. As I was very interested in Father Damien de Veuster and his work for lepers, we flew to the island of Molokai. Our guide, a Hawaiian who had contracted the disease as a child and who remembered the priest, showed us what is left of the priest's projects. For me, it was a spiritual experience to walk on Father Damien's grounds, pray in his church (St. Philomena), and meditate.

In California we visited Lloyd's cousin Virginia, whose husband was a professor of education at Stanford University. We spent a day and a night there and enjoyed a tour through this world-renowned institution of higher learning. Virginia wanted us to visit her brother Frederic in the seniors' residence in Boston and get acquainted with other Roberts families, most of whom he had never met. We experienced a most gracious welcome by some twenty members of the Roberts clan—most of them Harvard, Radcliff, or MIT graduates. Lloyd was very happy to have established the contact with his relatives with the help of his grandfather's autobiography.

In the same year, Lloyd became very unhappy with the way his company, Comalco Fabricators, was being led. As their sales manager, he wanted to reorganize and henceforth increase production, an effort his boss at first supported. On the fourth of July of that year, Lloyd received numerous phone calls from several sections of the company messaging him, "Yankee, go home!" He asked Bryan, his hypnotherapist, to help him cope with this stress. In the course of dealing with it, we considered moving to the United States, because Kaiser Aluminium, a part owner of Comalco, had a plant there. I consulted the *Higher Education Journal* and found an opening in my field of expertise at Austin College in Texas. I was invited to an interview there. What an experience! At breakfast in my hotel I was interviewed by the first dean, who then drove me to the college, where a series of further interviews were scheduled to take place. Several other deans, potential colleagues, students, and a cleaning lady asked me questions. After a discussion about my salary, I was asked if I had a question. Yes, I wanted to know how much a T-bone steak (my favorite meat) costs! Somewhat bewildered, I left Texas the next morning. On arrival in Adelaide, Lloyd and Peter, with his wife, Diana, were awaiting me. In order to come to a sensible decision in case the German chair was offered to me, Peter suggested to write all the pros and cons of a job change on a piece of paper. Well, I had never thought of anything like that, but it sounded most sensible. At the end of that exercise, the decision went in favor of *not* taking the position if offered. So the next day, I rang the college to withdraw my application. It turned out to be a wise decision, because six months later Lloyd became so terribly ill. I needed the support of all my colleagues in my department, a support I would never have been given so early after an initial appointment to my new position as chairperson of the German Department at Austin College. As a newcomer, I doubt that anybody would have taken over my responsibilities for six months without remuneration and then rearranged lecturing times to suit my needs, at the expense of their own comfort. There I experienced Australian mate-ship and readiness to help beyond financial matters and personal wishes, in other words, mate-ship at its utmost. You do not let a mate down, an attitude I came across quite often while living in Australia.

*****

The onset of Lloyd's illness and its consequences I described in detail at the beginning of these memoirs. After eight weeks of hospitalization in 1980, Lloyd was discharged from the AKH in Vienna and driven by ambulance to Bludenz. Soon after our return, our friend and neighbor Dr. Helmut Hutter arranged for Lloyd to be given reaction training in the neurological hospital of Vorarlberg, as he could not walk due to his inability to coordinate his arms and legs. Because Lloyd could not differentiate between day and night, windows and doors, Helmut visited us every evening at about nine o'clock, dressed in his white doctor's coat with a stethoscope around his neck and a glass of ghastly tasting sleeping medication (paraldehyde with raspberry juice) and gave it to my husband, as he refused to take it from me. We lived in my upstairs apartment and had great difficulties getting Lloyd into Helmut's car to drive him to his reaction training. Sometimes he insisted on going through the window instead of the door, which caused us a lot of problems. It was rather difficult to divert his thinking and make him do what was necessary. Little by little, the training and tranquillizing medication made it easier for me to look after him. Eventually I could take him with the help of his walking frame for short walks, but when he got tired, every car he saw was his, and he wanted to drive home. Once he was dead-set on getting into a car and got furious on the street because I prevented him from doing it. Then I noticed the first stars becoming visible in the sky. By talking to Lloyd about the stars, pointing at them, and singing a children's song about stars, I managed to move him and get him to walk home.

After eight weeks of successful training, the neurologist Professor Barolin issued him a certificate of fitness for air travel, which enabled us to return to Adelaide. We had a rather difficult flight, because Lloyd wanted to leave the plane in midair. He made his way to one of the emergency exits, politely asked to get to the door and tried to open it. I called the flight attendant to help me lead him back to his seat, but he insisted on getting off. Knowing that he responded to uniforms, I asked for the captain to come with his hat on. Thank goodness, he was as tall as Lloyd, so that they could see eye to eye. He advised the flight attendant to move the passengers from the last row of seats to make room for Lloyd, asked him to lie across the row of seats, and fastened him with seat belts. His head lay on my right thigh, and I gave him more Valium, which meant that I could not move from my seat. On advice of Professor Barolin, I had started to give him Valium already the day prior to our departure. We had to change planes in Bangkok, a harrowing ordeal; however, the flight attendants were most helpful in every respect. In Melbourne, my cousin Hans and his son Raimund, as well as Didy, were waiting for us to give us any assistance needed. Also waiting for us upon our arrival in Adelaide was the honorary consul, as well as an ambulance to take us home. Realizing that he would not be able to climb the steps to our upstairs bedroom, I had asked Didy to buy a folding couch for the living room for both of us to sleep on. A few days later, Dr. Dinning, the neurosurgeon at the Royal Adelaide Hospital, took Lloyd kindly into his care at his private hospital for the next three weeks to give me time to settle in at my university again and start looking for a more suitable house to buy.

*****

As mentioned before, our lives changed in every sense of the word after Lloyd had lost his memory, and no treatment and no effort I put into his recovery brought any result in that respect. It took me a long time to accept the new reality, particularly because no doctor in Australia gave me a shimmer of hope. Every one of them I consulted was most negative and tried to talk me into putting him into the Daws Road Repatriation Hospital, where patients of all ages—most of them suffering from frontal lobe damage (e.g., young motorcyclists and war veterans)—lived out their lives. When the neurosurgeon Dr. Dinning saw Lloyd for the first time shortly after our return to Adelaide, he told me he would never have operated on my husband. He would have simply let him die, because there was no hope of recuperation and no place for rehabilitation for him. I was devastated. After a few months, I seemed to have developed heart problems and went to see a cardiologist. He told me that Lloyd's behavior would be totally unpredictable—he might even kill me in a fit of anger. I did not believe him; I knew him better than anybody else on this earth. Yes, he smashed things, he threw objects through the kitchen, he dumped his lunch or dinner onto the floor, and he tore the zip of his trousers in the toilet when he could not open it at the first try. Once, for whatever reason, he destroyed the water container in the toilet. Much worse was to come.

In July 1980 my sister Ruth came to help us. At first, Lloyd was very happy with her presence. I felt free to work at the university and take driving lessons. Unfortunately I failed the driving test twice. It became necessary to sell our Spanish-style two-story townhouse and buy a bungalow-style one-story home that had a garden and a swimming pool. The latter had become necessary, because Lloyd still did not coordinate his arms and legs well when walking. Hans and Raimund joined us from Melbourne and drove us around Adelaide to find a suitable house. About three weeks after Ruth's arrival Lloyd began to hate her, because he realized that she was here to supervise him. The climax of his sudden dislike of her was reached when he threw her luggage through a window onto our car park, chased her out of the house, and went to the bus stop to go to the city. Ruth followed him every step of the way. He went into John Martin's, one of the large department stores, asking for employment; however, he only managed to write his name on the job application. Ruth got a hold of him and enticed him to go with her to the store's restaurant, promising him the biggest cup of ice cream the restaurant could offer. While he ate it, she phoned me at the university. My colleagues took over, and I could dash to the store and take Lloyd home, while Ruth stayed in the city. He told me that he would pack his things and join the US Navy again. Back home, I got him to sleep and then called the neuropsychologist. He offered to alert the airport and the harbor authorities, apparently unaware of the fact that only freight ships docked in our port. Ruth spent a few days with a friend to recover from her anguish, and, by getting her out of his sight, Lloyd forgot that she was there. I did not leave him alone with her again; instead, I organized some people to visit her and him while I was at work. Ruth returned to Austria after five weeks with us.

During the first year after our return, Lloyd suffered a heart attack and an infarct in the brain that necessitated hospitalization again. Several TIAs followed over the years. It was, of course, a setback to his health every time. One Saturday afternoon, Lloyd was busy breaking eight windows of our house with a stick, as I returned from a driving lesson. I had engaged his former workmate Clyde to look after him during my time with the RAA (Royal Automobile Association). To my surprise, Clyde left in a great hurry when he saw me return. He must have said or done something that had enraged Lloyd. What could I do? I knew that scolding him for his action was useless, as he did not know what he was doing. So I took him into my arms, assuming that he was very tired; led him into the house; took him into the bedroom; washed the perspiration off his face, hands, arms, and chest; covered him; kissed him; and wished him a good sleep. Then I dragged myself to the phone and rang our neuropsychologist. All he had to say was "We told you he belongs in Daws Road …," and when I asked him what I should do, his answer was very practical but cruel: "Get the glass company!" He was right with his second advice. Yes, I called the emergency window repairers, as it was Saturday early afternoon. When some time later Lloyd got up again, he had no idea why workmen were there.

Friends and acquaintances in the Austrian Club offered to help us. One day, Mr. Riedel rang the doorbell and suggested that he would look after our large back garden. He was divorced and lived alone despite having a bad heart condition. It was terrible for him and me when Lloyd became jealous and told the club members that he had to chase Mr. Riedel around the kitchen table, because he wanted to rape me. The poor man! I had to tell Mr. Riedel not to come again for a while, until one day when we saw him sitting alone at a table in the club. Lloyd felt sorry for him and asked me if we could invite him to sit with us. Obviously he had completely forgotten his previous behavior toward him and seemed to be his old self, friendly and welcoming. From then on I made sure to play "Ami rummy" (with five cards) or halma or children's games with Lloyd and—most important—let him win. For the next thirty-two years, I was the loser in most games! Not all the helpers I engaged in the course of his life in Adelaide and later in Bludenz could lose. Not winning made Lloyd so angry that he was likely to throw the cards through the room or turn the table over or, with a sweep of his arm, everything landed on the floor. His uncontrolled anger was scary for strangers—and was a test of my patience and understanding.

Lloyd showed an example of his anger in October 1981 in the AKH in Vienna, when Dr. Quatember wanted to test his cognitive abilities and asked him to perform a specific task with small blocks of wood. I was sitting outside of the examination room when I heard the noise of falling objects and someone speaking loudly, which made me wonder what might have happened. The doctor came out and told me that Lloyd had thrown all the blocks on the floor and now, on doctor's orders, was picking them up again.

Surprisingly, our neuropsychologist in Adelaide allowed Lloyd to drive our car. He had his driving license until 1986, when we had an accident returning from an evening in the club. A young man was speeding and ran into the back of our car. The doctor's reasoning for not revoking his license was: he had been driving all his life, so driving was stored in his long-term memory, and his deficiencies lay mainly in the loss of his short-term memory and his loss of local and time memory. He obviously had neither considered Lloyd's lack of self-control nor his impulsiveness. Therefore when his caregivers left before I returned from the university—I could not drive to work because I had no license at that time—it could happen that Lloyd drove to the city and parked our car somewhere, but he never knew where. It was most annoying for me to check every car park on North Terrace to relocate the car and then to argue with the car park authorities regarding unlawful parking. The solution to the problem was, of course, to speed up my obtaining the license. I passed the test on my third try. Looking back on it, I am glad Lloyd had no accident and no involvement with the police while he was driving to come to me. As mentioned in the first part of my memoirs, Bryan, his hypnotherapist, forbade him to drive for a while, at least until I had my license.

Every first Monday of the month, I brought Lloyd to the TPI House, where returned soldiers could spend a day together. Female and male returnees from the Australian Navy, Air Force and Army met to have a good time. The door opened at nine in the morning, and I had to pick him up no later than four in the afternoon. One day I dropped Lloyd off a few minutes before nine, as I had to be at a meeting at 9:00 a.m. sharp. I asked him to sit on a bench in the garden and wait for the person who would open up the building within five minutes. At about one in the afternoon, I received a call from the university's telephone operator who told me that someone was trying to locate me by phone. It was Lloyd. He did not know where he was. My shock was unimaginable! I found out that someone had given him a few coins to make the call. After many questions about what he could see and hear, I gathered that he was in Victor Harbor, a sea town some eighty kilometers away from Adelaide. Then he remembered that a bus had taken him there. My search for a bus company that had sent a bus to that town began. After awhile, I found the name of the company and managed to ask someone there to contact the driver, who should get in touch with me. Meanwhile, I got in touch with the local police in Victor Harbor and asked them to find my husband, find out the state of his mind, and, if necessary, take him to the local hospital to see if he was okay. A policeman from Adelaide should bring him back to Adelaide on his way home after work. As policemen have uniforms, and Lloyd had great regard for them as the defenders of law and order (after World War II he was a deputy sheriff in Tucson, Arizona, for seven months), he would not cause them any trouble. From the bus driver I found out that Lloyd had boarded a bus full of female senior citizens who were on a day trip to the sea. The bus had stopped in front of the TPI House due to traffic. Lloyd boarded the bus. He was the only man on board and, amazingly, nobody questioned his presence. As he had no money, a passenger paid for his lunch. Then the ladies dispersed, and he found himself alone. In the end, the driver offered to take him back to the TPI House along with the ladies and drop him off there, where I would be waiting for him. I found him to be in excellent spirits—he had had a great time!

There was another time when he could not find his way home. Our friend Harry and his wife, Lorna, spent the evening playing cards with us. At ten at night, they wanted to go home. Lloyd offered to drive them there. It meant driving down Maple Avenue to its end, then making a right turn and driving along the road to their house, a ride of about five minutes. When Lloyd had not returned an hour later, I rang them only to find out that he had dropped them off all right and then had presumably driven back. Full of worry, I contacted friends and neighbors to drive around and find him, but to no avail. I was hesitant to call the police, as they would rightfully have reproached me and at worst reported me to social services. In my despair, I prayed for his return. Sometime after midnight, he drove into our drive, while a car stopped in front of our house. I dashed out to talk to the driver, who told me that Lloyd had known neither where he was nor how he would get home. Lloyd had knocked at the man's front door, as he had seen a light burning in the house. The owner tried to explain to him the way back home, but he realized quickly that it was useless. So he drove ahead of Lloyd, having found our address in the telephone book. He had been in Gumeracha, some twenty-five kilometers in the Adelaide hills. None of our friends and neighbors would have tried to find him there in the middle of the night; neither would I have. Thank God, my sweetheart was brought back to me safe and sound. It was a huge lesson for me!

*****

Our life together could not go on like that. The medical world had nothing to offer me in terms of help. Some doctors even suggested getting a divorce so that I could pursue my career. I had to go to work at the university and find entertainers for Lloyd, as I was scared to leave my husband alone in the house. Friends and neighbors helped out for a while. I borrowed books from the university's medical school library and read as much about the brain as I could in an effort to understand his sick, his insured brain better. He quite often showed an amazing ability to cover up his memory deficiencies when we had company. In my despair, I wrote to Professor Reisner in Vienna, who answered me by return mail, suggesting that I bring Lloyd to him during my next stay in Europe. In his letter he also wrote, "I don't think that you should leave your husband. He needs much love and patience, and only you can give that to him." That visit occurred in the course of my study leave in 1981. We stayed again at Mario and Hanny's. I hoped in vain that Lloyd would recognize the place where he had suffered that insult to his brain, or at least remember our hosts. Mario took care of him while I spent time at the Boltzmann Institute and conferred with staff members at the Psychology Department of the university who, like me, were involved in studying brain-compatible learning in order to develop methods for increasing the pupils' memory capacity. My research not only benefited my students at Adelaide University, but it was to some degree also helpful in caring for Lloyd.

Prior to our leaving the AKH, Professor Reisner gave me some advice on how I could improve our situation. For him it was most important that Lloyd should spend some time in male company—so far mostly women were around him. Therefore, after our return to Australia, I arranged that Lloyd should join the Freemasons again, because the senior citizens' club I had gotten in touch with had rejected him. Harry Bateman, a friend I had met on the boat coming to Adelaide, and with whom we had stayed in touch, was most helpful in getting Lloyd reinstated with the Freemason lodge after he had obtained his clearance some twenty years earlier. I bought Lloyd the tuxedo he needed for the monthly meetings and a Freemason's ring as a Christmas present in that year. Harry or another brother from the lodge picked Lloyd up and brought him home after every meeting. My contribution to the lodge was my involvement in the roasting of three hundred sausages and lending a hand to other chores that needed to be done for every ANZAC Day meeting. Eventually I decided to join the women's branch of Freemasonry; after all, I wanted to know what Freemasonry stands for. I was most impressed by its members' involvement in social works, particularly by their erection of homes for the aged and by how they looked after the sick and infirm and helped anybody in need. Over the years, we benefited from their good deeds on numerous occasions, as for instance, every time Lloyd had a stroke and spent time in hospital, the almoner came to ask what he and the other brothers could do for us. While the almoner visited him in hospital, one or another brother came and helped me. Some brothers' wives brought me jams and fruits or vegetables to show me their support. When Lloyd's health deteriorated more due to infarcts in his brain, I considered making plans to move into one of the Masons' homes for the elderly. At one of their meetings, the plans for building a new senior citizens residence for Freemasons were presented.

The bungalows, the maisonettes, the nursing-home, and the gardens promised to be so beautiful, and the setting in between lots of eucalyptus trees and native bushes so lovely, that I put our names on a waiting list to be considered for acceptance. However, ultimately I could not see myself spending the rest of my life among senior citizens, many of them frail and sick, and thus I reluctantly—and Lloyd enthusiastically—decided to move back to Austria in due course.

One morning in 1984, I collapsed in my office. The staff physician to whom my colleagues brought me suggested getting in touch with social services in the city. A social worker came, assessed our situation, and went into action: I could bring Lloyd into a nearby day care center on three mornings every week at eight thirty and pick him up at four in the afternoon; an incontinency nurse was assigned to us, who visited Lloyd once a fortnight; when the day care centers were replaced by mobile caregivers, very kind women came to play cards with him (and let him win, of course); once a week a bus came at ten in the morning and took him along with other patients (in Australia they were called clients, not patients) to a church hall to play games and enjoy a cooked lunch, followed by a drive into the countryside. Afterward, they brought him home at three o'clock. Every year at Christmastime I joined them in the church hall, sang Christmas songs with the clients, and told them the story of "Silent Night." It was wonderful to see how their eyes lit up when I described the cold and the snow. All of them but one Greek man knew the texts of the songs from their childhood. In the day care center, Lloyd always sat with Mrs. Pfeifer, a lovely old lady who did not talk anymore. He held hands with her and told her stories of his involvement in the wars. When she was not there, he worried about her well-being and asked me to look after her. Sometimes he escaped and walked to the deli about sixty meters down the road to chat with Vince, a lovely Italian shopkeeper who gave him ice creams and chocolates, although he had no money on him, because he could not handle it anymore.

*****

I was frequently in touch with the Austrian Consulate and the embassy in Canberra to discuss the advantages and disadvantages of moving back home. I believe it was in 1996 that I was visited in our home by three members of the Austrian Ministry for Social Affairs, Ministerial Counsel Siedl, Director Linke, and Ms. Spiegel. They had come to Australia to visit all the Austrian Clubs in order to explain to their members the recent social security agreement that had been formalized between Australia and Austria, as many Austrians living in Australia (as well as many repatriates in Austria) were quite unhappy with it. They advised me to return home with Lloyd, where I still had my flat and relatives and friends to help me care for him. I was told that Lloyd's immigration to Vorarlberg would be easy, because soon immigration would become a matter for the individual states and no longer be a matter for the federal government.

In December 1997, I received a phone call from Canberra informing me that as of the first of January 1998, I could apply for a visa for Lloyd to immigrate to the state of Vorarlberg. For me, probably the worst year of my life in Australia began. On the advice of our physician, I placed Lloyd into the Adelaide Clinic, a private hospital that took only a dozen patients, with half a dozen doctors and nurses looking after them. I asked them to find out whether Lloyd really wanted to live with me in Bludenz. To me he said yes, he wanted to, but I was not sure if he understood what it meant to live in a country where he could talk to few people due to the language barrier. Lloyd had been there several times and loved it each time, but being a visitor or being a permanent resident were two different things. So I asked the doctors to find out what he wanted and tell me whether I should make the move. In that private clinic were a psychiatrist, a neurologist, a physician, an internist, a social worker, and specialized nursing staff, male and female. Lloyd was booked in for three weeks. To cover that time, I organized a number of friends and Freemasons to visit him, while I was busy giving lectures and seminars to teachers in other states of Australia. Besides, I took part in an all-day seminar, a course offered by the WEA (Worker Education of Australia) to learn how to sell one's house. I did not want just to rely on a real estate agent. Furthermore, I made lists detailing what contents of my house I wanted to sell, to ship to Bludenz, or to give to the Salvation Army. I selected one shipping company out of three, whose offers I had discussed with friends, as well as a real estate agent with a German background. For me it was also important that Lloyd would have Australian citizenship besides his American one, in case I died before him. A young relative living in Bludenz promised me to bring Lloyd back to Australia, and reliable friends in Australia gave me their word that they would look after his well-being, his finances, and his health, and visit him frequently. I drew up a will and last testament, which included my arrangements for Lloyd, and deposited it with my lawyer, a former student of mine. Lloyd became an Australian citizen on the thirty-first of March 1998. I sold my house on the second of April, and on the third of April, Lloyd suffered a stroke that incapacitated him to the point that he could not walk anymore.

A friend from the C. G. Jung Society—I was a member of it—came to my rescue. Lloyd spent the next two months in a private hospital on Pennington Road. I visited him daily for several hours and pushed the rehabilitation team to do the utmost for him. Sometimes Lloyd became very obstinate and difficult to handle. Dealing with me was also not easy, because I did not accept any excuses such as a shortage of therapists, which would have meant less rehabilitation for Lloyd. I told the staff manager, a very friendly Indian, to get a therapist from outside—after all, we were in a private hospital, and therapy was part of proper care for Lloyd. Two weeks before our planned return to Austria, Lloyd fell out of his bed and hurt his left elbow. He developed a bursitis that got infected by a combination of golden staph and so-called green bacteria and needed an operation. One day the orthopedic surgeon came with his nurse while I was visiting Lloyd. After checking the elbow and having a short conversation with me, he left telling the nurse to bandage the wound again. Minutes later I left, because I had a luncheon engagement. When I came back a good two hours later, the elbow had still not been bandaged. So I spoke to the nurse and learned that there were two types of nurses: those with a nursing diploma and—a new system of nursing training had just been implemented—those with a bachelor of nursing. The question arose: Who has to bandage the elbow, the nurse with the bachelor's degree or the one without? I was consternated and told them what I thought of this situation. I contacted the head of nursing, who sorted the problem out after I had left the room. I was told by one of them that I was a "commanding person." Never mind, Lloyd's elbow got bandaged!

The next problem concerned my own health. I had discovered a lump in my left breast and immediately lined up for a mammography. The lump was confirmed, and a biopsy was advised. Thank goodness, it turned out negative—no cancer!

In all my stress and strain, aggravated by Lloyd's stroke and my biopsy, there was one stroke of luck: the Dutchman who had bought my house was happy for me to stay in the house that no longer belonged to me, because he needed bridging finances to pay me. So we arranged that I could stay as long as was necessary for Lloyd to become fit enough to board a plane and leave Australia. However, I had to find an airline that would be willing to carry Lloyd. Only Malaysian Airlines agreed to take us after its physician had assessed a medical report from the hospital, and I had agreed to buy two one-way business-class tickets.

Then another problem arose. My cousin Hans came from Melbourne to see us off, although I had been in Melbourne in March to say good-bye. I picked him up at the airport to drive him directly to the hospital to visit Lloyd. On the way, somebody cut me off when I turned left at a corner and crashed into my car, a car I had sold only two days earlier. My cousin walked up and down the sidewalk murmuring repeatedly, "What an idiot! What an idiot!" The police arrived and tried to tell me that it was my fault. However, I knew that it was not. In the discussion, I found out that the culprit was a member of the Australian secret police. No wonder he did not want to be at fault! I rang up his boss who, like my cousin, said a few times, "What an idiot! Just wait until he comes to the police station!" He told me to have the car repaired and the bill sent to his office. The next hurdle for me was, of course, to inform the new owner, who had already paid for the car, of the accident. What a relief, he did not withdraw from the sale!

I spent my last three days in Adelaide at Vera and Victor's home, Vera having been my dentist all those years. For Hans, I arranged accommodation with Susi, my Serbian cleaning lady. On the morning of our departure, the airline sent a limousine for us to drive us to the airport. Shortly before its arrival, Lloyd had a bowel problem and needed to be showered and dressed again. Several nurses and orderlies busied themselves with him and his dirty clothes. How he got showered, his clothes washed and dried, and put on him again, I will never know. I was simply told to stay seated, put my hands into my lap, and try to relax. Everything else was managed by the most helpful hospital staff. When we arrived at the airport, fifteen friends and colleagues were waiting to see us off. Lloyd was put into a wheelchair, our friends surrounding him and giving him small gifts such as a little metal kangaroo and a small stuffed koala. Victoria, a tutor in our department at the university, was trying to handle our tickets, passports, and luggage, when the next problem arose. The stewardess on the ground insisted that we had too much luggage and was not willing to let it get through. On my request, she called the airline manager. Victoria told him of our imminent final departure from Australia and pointed at Lloyd, whose face was beaming with delight, because of all the attention he was getting from our friends, and at me, my face wet from all the tears I was shedding. That manager, a tall and strong man, must have been moved by that scene, because he said, "It's my birthday today … let them get through with everything." He ordered the ground stewardess to check our suitcases in. Then he grabbed my big traveling bag, which was filled with nappies for Lloyd, and took my arm to guide me out of the departure hall and onto the plane.

My farewell to Australia and leaving my life there behind me was—and still is—heartbreaking for me. On board, the manager assigned the strongest flight attendant to look after us in every way. I could see how touched that manager was about the whole situation, and I could not find words to thank him. So I gave him a hug and a kiss and whispered, "Thank you" … and he was gone. In my twenty-four years in Australia, I had met so many wonderful, compassionate, and helpful people as nowhere else. For me, the Australian expression "no worries" says it all: Don't worry, help is around the corner! No fuss made; lending a hand to someone in need comes natural. A thank-you is enough.

The flight went very well. Lloyd had to hold his right arm in a sling up in the air. The husky flight attendant moved him to the toilet whenever necessary. Besides, he came quite often to talk to him. In Kuala Lumpur, we had to change planes. The crew helped us in every way. All I had to do during the entire flight was look after my handbag. Before our arrival in Zurich, we received lots of presents from the purser, such as cosmetics, combs, little bottles of alcohol, a very nice leather wallet, which I am still using, and more. At the airport, my godchild Elsa and her husband were waiting to drive us to Bludenz and to a new life.

*****

In many ways, living in my apartment in Bludenz had lots of drawbacks compared to living in our house in Rostrevor. Here we have a flat, a cellar, an attic, and a garden; there we had had a bungalow-type house, a swimming pool, a front garden with roses, and a back garden with fruit trees and vegetables. Of course, the climate was also very different, hot in summer and cool in winter there; four seasons with comparatively cold winters in Bludenz. In Rostrevor, we could enjoy the hills, while Bludenz is surrounded by high mountains of up to three thousand meters. As my apartment is on the third floor in the house in Bludenz, it became obvious that we had to move to the ground floor as soon as possible. The fact that my youngest sister owned the lower two floors—both occupied by tenants—made life quite difficult for us. Lloyd fell frequently, which made it necessary for me to ask someone strong (i.e., any visitor or the tenant from the ground floor) to help me get him up. Besides, Lloyd could not get into our garden without extra help. We managed somehow for a year, when the ground floor tenant voluntarily moved out. Friends came and assisted me with the move downstairs. After having made adjustments to the bathroom, the kitchen, and the garden, which were necessary because of Lloyd's disabilities, our life became much more pleasant and comfortable.

*****

Now I will write more about my career and how it helped me cope with my husband.

In mid-May 1981, I was due for my second study leave. As far as walking was concerned, Lloyd had improved quite well, so that I could take him along to the United States, Austria, and West Germany. At Iowa State University in Ames, Iowa, I took part in Professor Donald Schuster's six-week summer school psychology course in suggestology and suggestopedia (teaching and learning with the use of suggestion). This course introduced me to a totally new and fascinating method of teaching and learning. The originator of this method was Professor Georgi Lozanov of Sofia, Bulgaria, who had developed it in the 1960s. In numerous Eastern Bloc countries of Europe, this method was used to accelerate learning in general and has been proven to be of special value to the learning of foreign languages. It reached the West in the early 1970s. I was particularly interested in the use of various kinds of music when teaching suggestopedically, an aspect that became very valuable for me in dealing with Lloyd. Over the next twenty years, Professor Lozanov and his master teacher, Evelina Gateva, and I became good friends and visited each other whenever they were in Vorarlberg. Through him, I learned to influence Lloyd's moods and his emotional outbursts and to give him back some self-confidence.

In Ames I went through a difficult time with Lloyd. Professor Schuster had allowed me to take my husband along to the lectures. Once during one of his seminars, Lloyd needed to use the toilet. I led him there and showed him the door to the lecture room where I was, because I did not want to miss too much of the work we were doing there. The toilet and the classroom were almost opposite each other and, in my view, hard to miss. However, after a while it occurred to me that Lloyd was taking a long time to return. Next to me sat a young man, a Franciscan father as I found out later, in civilian clothes. I asked him to look for Lloyd in the toilet. When he returned, he shook his head and whispered that he could not find him. That was obviously worrying and a good reason to interrupt the professor. Father Justin and I searched the building and the university grounds, but Lloyd was nowhere to be found. We contacted the university's campus security officers, who in turn also tried to find him, but to no avail. Suddenly I remembered a story Lloyd had once told me of a marine mate who became shell-shocked in the war in the Pacific and went lost. A search was undertaken, and the mate was found walking along the road of a village not knowing where he was. So I contacted the state troopers of Ames, gave them a description of Lloyd and his clothes, and asked them to look for him using their paddy wagon. They set off immediately. After some time, they found him walking along the highway, like his mate had done during the war, quite a distance away from the university, and brought him back in their wagon, just like a criminal. What a lesson that was for me! He could not be left alone for a minute! From then on, I hired a student, who had no afternoon lectures and was glad to earn some money, to entertain him daily for the three hours while I was engaged with my studies.

My interest in language methodology led me to the Mormon Language Training Center in Provo, Utah, and to the Brigham Young University in the same city. Until that visit, I had often wondered how young Mormons managed to learn different languages in a relatively short time. I sat in on several lessons, only to find out that these students who were being prepared for mission work in Europe and other parts of the world had to do an immense amount of rote learning. They basically learned large parts of the Bible and biblical exegeses by heart and practiced dialogues to be held with potential converts in their native languages. Clearly, the young Mormons make an immense effort to spread their faith!

In October 1981, during the second part of my study leave, I returned to Vienna on invitation from Professor Reisner. There I observed classes at the Boltzmann Institute for Learning Research and held discussions with teachers on their efforts to improve teaching and learning. Subsequently, I visited the Department of Psychology at the university, under whose guidance that research was conducted. During our stay in Vienna, we lived with our friends Hanny and Mario, who took care of Lloyd while I was working. Besides, I made time to reintroduce Lloyd to Professor Reisner,[†] Professor Quatember,[†] and Professor Koos[†] at the AKH, to get advice on how to help Lloyd and myself conduct our lives together—not realizing at all that I would be caring for him for the next thirty-one years.

Subsequently, my study leave took me to Germany. Lloyd was cared for by my friends in Wuppertal, while I attended lectures about the origin and development of the Federal Republic of Germany since 1945, delivered by Professor Schneider of the Department of Politics at the University of Munich, where I witnessed rather disturbing situations. He was often unable to begin his lectures until agitators of Spartakus, a Marxist student movement of that time, had finished presenting their unreasonable demands in the lecture hall.

The above represent just a few of my activities during that study leave period. Having participated in the psychology course at the university in Ames, Iowa, I realized that suggestopedic teaching incorporates several ideas I found to be helpful also in handling my husband. At the beginning of every lesson, there is a short period of relaxation. The appropriate music with guided imagery leads students into a desired calmness. The images used were mostly related to nature; for example, a walk along a beach was a favorite of mine and of Lloyd's. My Australian students had liked this imagery as well because Adelaide lies on the shores of the Southern Ocean, which made it easy for them to visualize the scene. I described a calming scene and asked the students to breathe in the cool sea air and breathe out anything that might be worrying them while watching the waves coming in, going out, listening to the seagulls and to the sounds of the waves, sitting in the sand and letting the cool sand run through their fingers, smelling the sea air, and so forth. Then I gave them some positive affirmations regarding learning. After a few minutes, I led them away from the beach and back into the seminar room. Other images I used were a walk in a forest, stepping into a cloud and sailing in the sky, while letting go of any trouble, worry, or anxiety (before a test or an examination) and thereby freeing their minds to be ready for learning. In the case of my husband, after such relaxation, I gave him positive affirmations such as "your wife loves you and looks after you," "you have no worries at all," "you are safe and happy," "you have many friends who love and visit you," "you are as well as can be," and more.

The images were accompanied by appropriate music i.e., nature sounds of the beach or birds in the woods, ethereal music for the sky, adagios of the classical and romantic periods. Over time Lloyd got so used to this treatment and enjoyed it to the point of missing it when I thought I did not have time for him. I produced a tape, which I called "Music, Imagery and Relaxation" (in the early '80s there were no CDs) that the university sold to the public.

The benefits of music for brain-injured persons became very clear and convincing to me, especially when I realized that I could change Lloyd's moods by playing the pieces he responded to at specific times. He was very musical, loved the classics and the romantic pieces, disliked Baroque music (only since his illness), hated the organ because it "confused" him, loved the piano and the string instruments, and above all, responded to singers, particularly to Pavarotti, with great enthusiasm. Once at home in Bludenz he insisted on going to the Austrian Club—he did not realize that he was not in Adelaide—and became very violent toward Agi, one of his Slovak caregivers, and me. He sat in his wheelchair trying to get himself to the apartment door, and yelled and fought us, grabbed the nearby telephone and threw it onto the floor. We were at a total loss about what to do with him until Agi had a brain wave: she put a CD with Pavarotti on the player … and Lloyd calmed down instantly and, with love and admiration in his eyes, said, "Isn't he wonderful!" In that particular incident, Agi and I were too involved with trying to reason, even fight with him about why he could not go to the club instead of staying calm and diverting his thinking.

At times, when he was restless or could not go to sleep, his caregivers or I played soft music such as adagios by Italian, French, German, or Austrian composers on tapes and CDs for him. This worked quite often better for him than tranquillizers or sleeping tablets, particularly in the early years of his illness.

When Lloyd was depressed, I played our CDs with the Vienna New Year's concerts or our videotapes with Kiri Te Kanava, a wonderful Maori soprano from New Zealand, whose body language while singing is most captivating and entertaining. The musical *Singing in the Rain* with Fred Astaire also lightened his mood as well as American military music. We listened to music while playing cards with him; in fact, there was hardly a time when no music was playing in our home. He could not bear most modern music and turned verbally nasty at the sound of any type of rock, let alone heavy metal. Even most jazz he could not condone, unless it was Dixieland music from New Orleans. Once we went to Feldkirch (Vorarlberg) to listen to a concert. The last piece was a composition of a contemporary musician. Lloyd became restless and angry. At the end of it, he got up and yelled out of control, "This is the worst load of BS I have ever heard in my life." It was terrible for me. I took him by his hand and led him out of the concert hall apologizing all the way. It was the last live concert I attended with him.

We listened to/watched many operas on TV. To my amazement, not understanding the text did not worry him much for many years. I just had to tell him the gist of what was going on, because he concentrated on the music and the singers. Only in the last few years of his life he asked repeatedly while watching an opera, "What are they saying?

And he lost patience with sitting in front of the TV screen, unable to follow either the story or the music. He preferred to go to sleep.

*****

In 1983, prior to my next study leave, my university gave me short-term conference leave to accept an invitation by Professor Machado of the University of Rio de Janeiro to speak at a conference of university language teachers and conduct a seminar afterward. Our doctor encouraged me to accept, because she was able to make arrangements for Lloyd to be looked after in a private psychiatric hospital during the time of my absence. Besides, she thought it would do me good to have a break from looking after him. When I brought him to the hospital, it took him no time to find card players among the young female patients, while a male nurse tried to dispel any worries I had regarding my leaving him for three weeks and traveling so far away. After the conference, which lasted for a week, I gave a demonstration of suggestopedic teaching at a post-conference workshop followed by several hours of lecturing. The conference organizers had planned some excursions for the participants, which I used for networking with new colleagues, while enjoying the Sugar Mountain, the Copacabana, and other sights. I was robbed at a market on the Copacabana during my bartering with a salesman from whom I wanted to buy a handcrafted flute made by Indios. Meanwhile, my handbag had been slit the full length, and my wallet containing money, my hotel safe key, and my American Express card were stolen. I still cannot understand how this could have happened without me noticing anything. In the police station, an officer told me that if I had noticed it while it happened, I might not be alive anymore. That experience put quite a damper on my enthusiasm for Brazil. On my way back to Adelaide I stopped in Arlington to study the American version of suggestopedia along with some colleagues from the Rio conference in a one-week course. There a guest room in our hotel caught fire during one night and all of us had to evacuate. When I came home, Lloyd was as happy as a lark because he had had such lovely company. The young apparently depressed patients told me that Lloyd had done them more good than all the psychiatric nurses together. Shortly after our arrival at home, I received a phone-call. A real estate agent wanted to inspect our house with the intention of purchasing it, because Lloyd had told him that we would move to Austria and would therefore sell our house. He mentioned that Lloyd had offered it to him for $60,000—which was several times under the going price. My husband had presented himself to this agent definitely not as a patient, although he had wondered why the price was so low. It was hard to leave Lloyd without my supervision.

*****

In 1984, my next study leave from the University of Adelaide took me first to Perth, Western Australia, where the first National Convention of the Accelerative Learning Association (ALSA) took place. In the year before, I had conducted a three-day seminar on accelerated learning in that city. More than a hundred people, many teachers among them, had come to participate and afterward enrolled in my postconference workshop. One outcome of the convention had been the creation of ALSA, of which I was elected president. A number of teachers from other Australian states had become very interested in Professor Lozanov's teaching method and imported that interest into their schools. At the convention, I gave several lectures and research reports concerning my first suggestopedic German course, which I had held at the University of Adelaide, and about my privately conducted course in New South Wales.

At one of the conferences I had attended and spoken at in the United States, I met Professor Hideo Seki, who invited me to visit Japanese universities and experience their adaptation of suggestopedia. Therefore, after Perth, I returned to Adelaide to prepare lectures for my visit to Japan, where I spoke to the language teachers at Sanno and at Tokai University, and held conferences with language teachers in Kyoto and Shin Kurashin. In Kyoto, I met one of the participants from Professor Schuster's psychology course in Ames, Iowa. Ostrander & Schroeder's book *Superlearning* had reached Japan and was being hotly and critically discussed by Japanese language teachers. Japanese suggestopedia differed markedly from Eastern Bloc and Western suggestopedia, partly due to the totally different music. In Tokio, the teaching staff of Tokai University invited Lloyd and me to a most interesting meal. I had to "pinch" Lloyd several times during the meal, when he wanted to tell our hosts that he had been in the Pacific war fighting the Japanese. Because Lloyd's brain had lost its critical barrier as a result of his subarachnoidal hemorrhage, his compulsion to blurt out whatever came into his mind at any moment meant that it became quite often embarrassing to have him in company.

In Shin Kurashin, we stayed with a family in a house that seemed to be made of paper. It had a large living room, where the family of five, joined by ten of their friends and /or relatives, Lloyd and I, as well as Armand, a Canadian acquaintance of mine from the metaphysical society, had dinner together. We sat on the floor (Lloyd and I had cushions), holding a bowl and chopsticks in our hands. We ate fish, rice, and some large green leaves, and drank tea. Nobody talked, because most people around the table could not speak English. We just bowed to each other and smiled. We found our hosts to be most polite. After the meal, we moved into a music room, where I noticed the most up-to-date hi-fi equipment. Our host showed us LPs with mostly European Baroque music such as Bach and Handel. A rolled-up newspaper with something that was definitely not tobacco was lit and passed around. Armand, sitting next to me, whispered that Lloyd should definitely not smoke it when it came around to him. I let it pass me, too. Nobody spoke; everybody listened to Bach or Handel while having a draw of whatever it was. Eventually I noticed that one person after the other disappeared, and when they reappeared they were red as lobsters. Again Armand did not want Lloyd to "disappear," but I went, as I was curious to find out what it was in which Lloyd should not participate. It was a Japanese bath. I had to wash myself with soap before stepping into the very hot water in the bathtub, where I was to sit quietly for ten minutes. After getting out, I had to take a cold shower, dry myself, and join the group in the music room again. Of course, I was as red as a lobster like all the others who had gone through the ceremony.

Fortunately Lloyd did not indicate that he wanted to go where I had been, so I took his hand, bowed to everybody, and climbed the small steps up to our bedroom. We slept on a thin mattress on the floor with only a neck roll under the head. In the morning, breakfast was eaten in a beautiful garden with about twenty or more neighbors, all sitting on little statues (houses, bridges, mushrooms, tables, etc.) made of stone or concrete, bowing and smiling at each other. Again, out of politeness as Armand explained to us, nobody spoke, no music was played, no sounds but for the singing of birds. I noticed five houses like the one of our hosts, where neighbors lived. Our breakfast consisted of thick slices of toast, green leaves like those at the evening meal, hard-boiled eggs, and tea. Our host's wife sat about half a meter above ground on the floor of the open door and served us what we wanted, every time bowing and smiling. After the meal, our host took eight of us guests in his Toyota Minivan to a beautiful park, where we saw large koi swimming in little streams and where we visited a pagoda and a Samurai temple. Toward the evening of that day, we returned to Tokyo by one of those famous very fast trains. After another night in our hotel in Shin Kurashin, a suburb of Tokyo, we embarked on the next leg of my study leave. Armand accompanied us to Narita airport for our flight to Copenhagen via Alaska. We enjoyed our five-hour stopover in Anchorage and admired the beautifully hand-knitted pullovers and coats made of lamb's wool as well as handcrafted knickknacks made of reindeer horns.

I knew that in Denmark suggestopedic teaching was well known. I was mostly interested in the Institute for Educational Development, where one of my international conference colleagues taught Danish to tortured and jailed refugees that had been freed by Amnesty International. I was told that because conventional teaching methods had mostly failed, some teachers had turned to the Lozanov method and were succeeding with it.

In Stockholm, Uppsala, and Tierp, I contacted several Swedish teachers, who taught not only languages but also other subjects with the suggestopedic method, researching its effectiveness. In Tierp, I watched Bulgarian and American videotapes and noticed the differences in style. A teacher from Tierp had been allowed to visit Professor Lozanov in Sofia several times and registered an institute in Sweden called Stiftelsen Pedagogisk Utveckling. Lloyd and I were his guests for several days.

The greatest interest in suggestopedia I found in Finland. Finnish teachers had founded a professional society based on the Lozanov method already in 1982 (in Australia in 1983). In Helsinki and in Oulu, I became acquainted with a version of this method that suited the Finnish culture.

As I had combined conference leave (two weeks), study leave (three months) and annual leave (five weeks) with my long service leave (three months), I was away from my university for quite some time. That enabled me to travel to Norway and visit the Maritime Military War Museum in Narvik, where I gained insight into the horrible happenings during World War II. I came across a distinct dislike of anything German, as the population of that city had suffered tremendously—the city was mostly destroyed by the German military in April 1940. On our way south, we spent a few days in Trondheim, where we had the opportunity to listen to a wonderful organ concert in the city's famous cathedral.

It was rather strenuous for me to have Lloyd in tow with me on all these travels, although my Scandinavian colleagues and Armand in Japan had done their utmost to entertain him and look after him when I was professionally engaged. Lloyd needed a lot of attention; he could not be sidelined, he did not want to hear "teacher talk" most of the time, and he got tired out by visiting one Japanese temple after another with my Japanese colleagues and friends, who wanted us to see as much as possible of their country. For instance, on our way to Shin Kurashin, we wanted at first to continue the long train trip to Hiroshima, but about half an hour before our train would have arrived there, Lloyd got up and said that he did not want to see Hiroshima. I think the fact that the first atomic bomb was dropped on Hiroshima by the US Air Force must have entered his mind, and he could not cope with that at that moment. So we got off the train at Shin Kurashin. I believe, if Armand had not been with us every day while in Japan, Lloyd would have caused me a lot of trouble. In Scandinavia, my colleagues were well prepared for him and had assigned students to look after him under the pretext that they had to practice their English with him. In Japan, I was not sure that I could leave him alone with any Japanese.

When we finally arrived in Bludenz, I was so exhausted that I ended up in the local hospital for two weeks. Meanwhile, my husband was looked after by my youngest sister. After discharge, I rested in my flat for another week, before I continued my work at the Boltzmann Institute for Learning Research in Vienna. Dr. Vanacek of the

Department of Psychology at the University of Vienna had developed his own accelerative learning program for mathematics, which contained elements of the Lozanov method for language learning.

In general, I noticed a remarkably greater interest in suggestopedia in Europe than during my previous study leave. In Liechtenstein, several teachers were trained in this method to use it experimentally in the upper school in Vaduz. I found great interest at the University of Heidelberg and at the Technical University of Heilbronn, where I was invited to hold a seminar for students.

Connected to the Karl-Marx-University in Leipzig, then East Germany, a scientific research laboratory within the Institute of Mnemology had been established. At the time of my first visit, its study focus was on music. The effects of various kinds of music and the bodily responses to it were researched in detail. I met Dr. Dieter Lehmann, a music specialist, who, with Dr. Jänicke, a neurologist, and several language teachers, had conducted the research. I was invited to observe Spanish language classes for a whole week—Cuban Spanish was taught—and received an extensive report about the project. In time, I translated much of that report and commented on it by including some of my own observations in an English publication. While I was in the GDR, Lloyd was looked after by my friends in Wuppertal. He could not have coped with a communist country due to his brain damage—his loss of the control barrier in his brain. For me, my one week stay in Leipzig proved to be the highlight of my research for the rest of my active teaching life. However, I felt uncomfortable once I noticed that I was being observed and followed by an agent whenever I walked on the street, even when I entered the St. Thomas Church to listen to a Bach concert—J.S. Bach had been the organist and choir director there for many years. Ultimately, Dr. Lehmann suggested that I should leave the GDR. A year later, we met again in Reading, England, where he could present his research, and I could sell my translation into English.

On our way back to Australia, we stopped in Ames, Iowa, where a SALT (Suggestive Accelerative Learning & Teaching) conference was held. There I viewed numerous videos on accelerative learning as practiced in the United States. I noticed the method being adapted, changed, watered down, "improved" as some people called it, and infiltrated by "new age" ideas. In several countries in Europe, accelerative learning societies were established (e.g. in Great Britain, France, and Germany). Many aspects of the Lozanov method eventually became absorbed in conventional teaching. To me, the interest in suggestology and suggestopedia showed that a dire need existed to change education in schools, to change the way students were supposed to learn; the hidden potential that lies in the learners' brains needed to be stimulated; more emphasis needed to be placed on the development of the learners' creativity; interest in the material they had to learn needed to be instilled so that school was a place for **all** to enjoy, teachers as well as pupils/students, and much more. However, suggestopedic teaching makes considerably more demands on teachers in terms of preparation and delivery of the teaching materials. In many countries of the Western world, conferences on accelerative learning took place and were attended each time by hundreds of teachers and educators. Until the fall of the Iron Curtain, Professor Lozanov and his master teacher Evelina Gateva were rarely allowed to present their ideas in Western countries because certain parts in politics had unreasonable expectations of the ultimate effectiveness of Lozanov's research efforts. At a number of language conferences (including the United States and Australia) I came across delegates from the military, who showed a particular interest in suggestopedia.

Ever since 1975, there has been a tremendous surge and interest in neurological research. At every conference on suggestology and suggestopedia I have ever attended worldwide, neuroscientists were present and spoke at these conferences about the brain and its functions and potential. I myself would hardly have delved so deeply into this subject matter, had my husband not had the brain damage he suffered on the thirtieth of January 1980. That event and its outcome gave my life a new direction, a new interest that helped not only my students, but also my brain-damaged husband.

The year 1985 was occupied by preparations for the second ALSA conference, to be held in Perth in November of that year. Directly after the conference, in February 1986, I was elected chairperson of the German Department at Adelaide University. With the support of Vice Chancellor Donald Stranks,[†] I invited two American medical educationists, one from the University of Illinois and one from the University of Southern California, to visit Adelaide University under a short-term Fulbright program. A colleague from our Conservatorium of Music, an educational psychologist, as well as a PhD student from Flinders University in Adelaide, joined me and the two

American guests to discuss accelerative teaching methods and the possibility of interdisciplinary research.

In the second half of 1986, I was due for my fourth study leave, which was to begin with a project in South Africa. The question was what to do with Lloyd? A young man from my neighborhood in Austria was spending some time in Australia and visited us for a few weeks. He agreed to accompany Lloyd back to Austria so that I would be free to go to South Africa. However, in spring of 1986, Lloyd contracted the so-called Legionnaires' Disease (an atypical pneumonia) in the day care center in Adelaide that he visited a few days every week. He was hospitalized for two weeks. As many patients in the United States and in Australia had died of it, I was most concerned. This at that time hardly known disease had received its name because a number of legionnaires caught it while they were at a conference in Philadelphia. At first nobody knew why this outbreak had happened, but in due course it was found out that the bacteria that caused it came from the hotel's air conditioners. Would Lloyd be well enough to undertake the long flight from Adelaide to Zurich, the closest airport to Bludenz? By the time I had to be at Stellenbosch University, Lloyd was able to fly. Until my arrival in Bludenz from South Africa two weeks later, a relative stayed with him in my flat.

*****

I had been asked to serve as external examiner of a PhD thesis on suggestology and suggestopedia at Stellenbosch University in South Africa and also to conduct the student's defense of it. At that time, Stellenbosch was the only South

African university that accepted so-called "coloured" students and staff. The candidate, Ludolph Botha, was very well prepared; his thesis was very good, therefore we had no problems. I had never been on the African continent before, so I was most curious to find out what would await me there outside the campus. The staff of the Education Department was most hospitable and spoiled me beyond imagination. I was shown many interesting parts of the Cape region and told a great deal about South Africa's past and present history. Every day one staff member took me to lunch in a fabulous restaurant situated in an old-time winery somewhere out in the country with Indian service personnel clad in Indian clothes. I tasted different world-famous Cape wines and ate the best local food of Dutch, English, and Indian origin. One professor took me to the Africaans Monument, which stands on a hill and was erected in recognition of Africaans as a language in its own right. Another colleague showed me the remarkable Huguenot cemetery. Unfortunately, the Table Mountain had a hat on so that the view was not good enough to enjoy. I gave lectures at the university and at both Denneord and Cape Town Teachers' Colleges, where I spoke to all aspiring young teachers, and, according to both directors of the two colleges, I instilled a lot of enthusiasm into these future colleagues for their chosen profession. The university had planned to take me to Mozambique, but because of unrest among parts of the population, that excursion had to be canceled. Instead I flew directly to Zurich, where Lloyd and his caregiver were waiting for me.

During my study leave in Europe, I followed up on my previous research in Vaduz and Leipzig. In Finland,

I conducted a one-week seminar for language teachers in Helsinki and lectured and observed classes in Oulu, Torneo, and Rovaniemi. In Rovaniemi, the wife of the governor of Finnish Lappland drove Lloyd and me the eight kilometers to Santa Claus, who lives on the Arctic Circle. Standing there in the snow in the pitch dark, we noticed Santa's dozen reindeer and his sleigh ready for their ride to the children of the world. Then we entered Santa's house, where he and his brownies, wearing their red caps, live and work. Lloyd enjoyed talking to Santa Claus, who, of course, was dressed in his Santa robe, and to his brownies, who help him answer Christmas mail from all over the world, including Japan and Moslem countries. We did not know that Santa was married (!), when we were introduced to Mary (Merry) Christmas! Santa gave us twenty letters we should write to him with the addresses of friends. He (or his brownies) would answer and mail them from Santa Land. Nobody who actually received such a letter could guess correctly why they had been on Santa's mailing list! Just before departing, we saw lots of cars racing by us and were told that tire companies tested tires at the Arctic Circle, particularly in early winter. Our host driver told us that Eleanor Roosevelt had been in that area shortly after World War II and had seen the devastation of Rovaniemi—only one prewar house is left; the entire town was destroyed in World War II. That building had become a souvenir shop by the time we were there.

Our next stop was West Berlin, where I spent some time with Professor Ludger Schiffler at the Free University. He had produced several videotapes with suggestopedic language teaching. During our short stay there, we lived in my cousin's apartment. He showed us the Berlin Wall and took us for a walk along the wall. Lloyd became anxious when he saw Checkpoint Charlie and the East Berlin observation towers along the wall. When he noticed the machine guns on the towers, he became so frightened that we had to leave the area. It must have reminded him too much of the wars he was involved in: World War II and the Korean War. Back in Bludenz for the turn of the year, I gave a four-hour presentation about suggestopedic teaching to my former colleagues at the Teachers College in Feldkirch before returning to Australia again.

In 1988, I took part in the International Linguistics Congress, which was held in East Berlin and lasted for five days. More than fifteen hundred linguists from around the world were present, over fifty delegates alone from Russia. Linguistics was divided into twenty different areas of research. For me it was most stimulating to meet numerous colleagues from various parts of the world who concentrated their research efforts on language issues and language-related fields. At the Congress dinner, ten delegates sat at my round table, including my friend Dr. Lehmann from Leipzig and another East German, one Russian, and one delegate from Poland. Before the end of the Congress, I received a telegram from Professor Miodunka of the Jagiellonian University with an invitation to come to Cracow. I had met him first in the department of sociology in Adelaide, where he had been a guest for some time. In East Berlin, I had the privilege to stay with Dr. Lehmann in his son's house, which was much more pleasant than staying in a building for university students. On one afternoon during the Congress, we were invited by the organizers to a most relaxing boat ride down the river Spree. Next to me sat a colleague from Poland. After a lengthy discussion about Frederic Chopin, he presented me with an LP from the last Chopin competition, where young piano competitors gave their best. At the end of the Congress, we delegates could choose a two-day guided excursion in the vicinity of East Berlin. I chose Saxony and its mountains, the Sächsische Schweiz. My travel partner was Mihail, a Russian linguist with a great sense of humor and impeccable German. At the beginning of our conversation, I thought that he was East German, because I could not detect the slightest indicator that would have given him away as being anything else than a Saxon, when he spoke either German or the Saxon dialect. However, later on he told me that he was Russian and the director of Russian language instruction in all schools of East Germany. He had learned German at the Pushkin Institute in Moscow. That, of course, reminded me of my visit to the US Defense Languages Institute in Monterey, California, where American military students learned impeccable German and a German dialect.

*****

In 1989, the focus of my next study leave started with the preparations for the fourth National ALSA Convention, followed by my postconvention workshop. Later, Lloyd and I traveled to Superior, Wisconsin, where I gave several lectures at the university. In Reading, UK, I chaired three sessions held by my co-researcher, Dr. Lehmann, on the use of music in suggestopedic teaching. There I almost lost Lloyd, who entertained himself with two female conference participants. Fortunately, I overheard these two ladies inviting him to accompany them to London in the evening. They did not realize his mental state, as he could present himself very well and hide his health problems. So I introduced myself to them and led my husband away. After the conference I took part in a two-week seminar conducted by Professor Lozanov and Evelina Gateva in Tierp, Sweden, while Lloyd was looked after by the organizer's wife and family, who had invited us to stay in their house.

*****

The problems I had been faced with every time I had taken Lloyd abroad needed a solution. I wondered whether it would not be better to reduce my overseas engagements and leave Lloyd cared for in Adelaide. The decision was made for me, when during my next leave period in 1991 Lloyd suffered a heart attack while in Bludenz and had to spend some weeks in our local hospital. After his discharge and a period of recovery in my hometown, our neighbor and friend Dr. Hutter insisted on driving us to Macerata, Italy, where I, as one of nine experts from nine different countries, presented two papers on suggestopedia. Dr. Hutter looked after my husband during our five-day stay there. I suggested that in case Lloyd gave him any problems, he should buy him the biggest ice cream available, and then he would settle down. Dr. Hutter did just that. The University of Macerata was celebrating its seven hundredth year of foundation. On our way there, Dr. Hutter wanted to stop in Loreto for a few hours. On the square in front of the Basilika, sick people and invalids in wheelchairs arrived with religious and Red Cross nurses for an outdoor Mass. Lloyd could not understand what was going on and felt very uneasy at the sight of hundreds of wheelchairs and even beds with patients being pushed by nuns in their, for him, strange habits. It must have impressed him very much, because on our return drive to Bludenz, we stopped in Assisi, where, when he saw a busload full of Americans standing in front of Saint Francis's Basilika, he told the people that a miracle had made him walk again a few minutes ago and that he was waiting for another miracle to make it possible for him to climb the winding steps down to the lower level of the church. I saw lots of cameras clicking and people saying, "Imagine, we have just seen the latest miracle of Saint Francis!" I did not know, should I laugh or cry? I just led him gently away. Then I remembered what I had told him in Loreto, where he had seen all these sick people waiting for a miracle to get healed. It was the last time for me to take Lloyd overseas. I had to accept the fact that people like Lloyd with frontal lobe damage create their own reality and do not remember what they say.

*****

In 1993, my last period of study leave prior to my voluntary retirement in 1994, I spent a part of the time lecturing in Sydney at the Deputy Principals' and Leading Teachers' Conference of NSW. Afterward, I flew to Europe to follow up on recent developments in the research on the reserve capacities of the brain/psyche in Berlin and in several places in Austria and in Liechtenstein.

In the course of my study leaves, I learned a great deal not only about teaching more effectively but also about the human brain. My studies took place at a time when brain research was moving to the forefront of medical research in about 1975. In every conference I took part in or just attended, there were always a few neuroscientists whose lectures and discussions sought to connect ongoing brain research with advancements in education, and also stressed the importance of applying music to teaching and healing. For me, it was the ideal time not only for enhancing my teaching, but particularly for helping my brain-injured husband and thereby making our life together possible till my husband's death on the seventeenth of July 2012.

......

As mentioned earlier, upon our return to Bludenz in May 1998, life was rather difficult in the beginning. Once we could move to the ground floor, we were more mobile. Lloyd and I managed to make use of our garden on sunny days. Our wonderful neighbors, Austrians as well as Turks, were on standby to help at any time. I had to take a practical driving test, because Australians drive on the left side of the road, whereas Austrians (as the rest of continental Europe) drive on the right side. It took me five driving lessons to get used to it. I bought a second-hand car, which made shopping and visiting my sister in Feldkirch easier. For Lloyd, I bought an indoor walking frame and a rollator for outdoors, which he used for a few years. However, little by little his condition worsened, and we needed a wheelchair. The only outside help I had for Lloyd at this time was provided by the local district nursing society, which came three times a week to shower him.

For the school year of 1999/2000, I offered accommodation to an American Fulbright student from Atlanta, Georgia, to thank the Fulbright Commission for my two years in New York. Lloyd and I had a great time with

Josh. He was a teaching assistant at the local high school. Every Friday, I invited him to lunch, while on other days he was either invited out, or he cooked his own meals. While Lloyd had his afternoon sleep, Josh and I had a discussion on his week at school and on his life and future in general. By explaining our dialect to him, he developed an interest in philology, one of my favorite subjects. Before he left, I gave him a book and a CD on the Alemannic dialect. In his first mail to me from home, he wrote of his decision to study German philology for his PhD. On my recommendation, he applied for a semester in Iceland to study the Icelandic culture and get introduced to the Icelandic language.

Similarly, during our time in Australia, we had also often invited children of my Austrian friends and relatives to stay with us and attend school in Adelaide or to use us as a base for traveling around Australia. As they came during their summer holidays, and school was in session in Adelaide at that time, I could send the younger ones to school. They enjoyed school and found it very different from schools in Bludenz and Feldkirch. The primary school, as well as the secondary school, was in our neighborhood in Adelaide, so they could walk there easily. I also arranged for them to do sports: football (soccer), rugby, and tennis—and, of course, cricket. In the eight weeks they spent with us, they learned English very well, as they were involved with Australian children all day. Besides, in our house only English was spoken. Whatever they wanted, they had to ask for it in English. I gave them that rule as soon as we picked them up at the airport. On weekends, we took them on trips to show them South Australia. One boy I took to Canberra, another one went with us on a cruise in the South Pacific, and two of them we showed the opal mines in Coober Pedy, and afterward we flew on to Ayers Rock.

In November 1999, a year and a half after our return to Austria, having overworked myself with the move back and bearing the responsibility for Lloyd all day, I suffered a breakdown and spent nine days in our local hospital. According to my neurologist, I suffered from burnout. He advised me to engage the mobile help service to give me some free space. It was very difficult to find anybody because of the language barrier between Lloyd and any possible helpers. After several unsuccessful tries through the director of this service, I decided to organize the necessary help myself and began to tell friends and acquaintances about my needs. By being direct and outspoken, I finally found and employed the women I needed: middle-aged, with compassion and understanding and unafraid to use the knowledge of English they had acquired in our schools. Junior secondary school English was good enough! Lloyd liked them all, and they liked him, because he paid everyone a compliment every time they came: on a necklace or a blouse or their hairstyle ... and if he could not find anything special, he told the lady that she had a lovely smile, a smile that lit the room up. He was very good at complimenting ladies. The women who came to play cards with Lloyd and who—very importantly—were prepared to lose the game most of the time, usually stayed for two to three hours a time. That gave me time to shop or meet a friend for a cup of coffee or simply relax.

These arrangements were a big help to me, but they proved not to be enough. After a few years of diminishing health, it had become too much for me physically as well as emotionally to cope with Lloyd's needs. My neurologist advised me urgently to look for twenty-four-hour care. I was incredibly lucky to find a series of wonderful young women in Slovakia who over the next eight years took turns staying with him until he died. Katarina was so intelligent that after a good year with Lloyd, I insisted she go to university to study. She chose andropedy (adult education) first, and later sociology, and ended her studies with two master's degrees. Lucia was not interested in studying, as she had other plans, and stayed on after Katarina had left. She found another Slovak "girl," Jana, to swap with her every three weeks, until Jana got married. I made arrangements for Lloyd, so that I could be present at her very beautiful traditional wedding in Slovakia. Petra had a master's degree in law but no job, so she took Lucia's place in due course. I encouraged her to continue her studies toward a doctorate. She reached her goal in 2014, while working in the police department. Natalia stayed for a year, when she got pregnant, and I suggested that she should stay with her family.

Anina and Agi were with us the longest, both until Lloyd's death. It was Anina's turn to go home on the morning when Lloyd left us. Lucia was here, and Agi took Anina's place to help out, because I was on respite, ordered by my physician. Our family doctor and the palliative care nurse told me that both girls had been absolutely wonderful before and after his passing away. They rang the doctor; the nurse; Annelies and her son, Wolfram, and informed my neighbors. My "girls" washed his body three times, dressed him, and tidied up his room. Annelies brought flowers and laid them on his body. When the undertaker came, the girls put his favorite mascot into his coffin. Several times every day during her last two fortnights before Lloyd died, Anina sat by his bedside and read him the psalm of the *Good Shepherd,* Lloyd's favorite biblical text, because it quieted him down when he was restless. Anina told me only recently that on that last morning before she left to catch the train back to Slovakia, she spoke to him about his leaving us soon; she even said that he could leave, if he wanted to go. Anina left; Agi arrived shortly thereafter, and an hour later he stopped breathing.

As I said, we had wonderful young Slovak women helping us. I cannot thank all of them enough, including those such as Natalia, Lubica, Martina, and Zuzana, who helped out when the "regulars" could not come for any reason. Each one was different, but each one did her best to make Lloyd's and my life easier. We did our best to show our appreciation. Lloyd left us over three years ago, and the "girls" and I are still in touch with each other. All the regular girls I mentioned here came the long way (fourteen hours by train each way) from Lucenec in the middle of Slovakia to his funeral. During the funeral Mass, Agi read the eulogy Anina had written for him, and standing in the front of the presbytery, each one of my "girls" read a short prayer we had written together. They followed the coffin, carrying his photo and their lovely flower arrangement, to the cemetery. They came again, when I had my eightieth birthday last year. For me, they are "the daughters I never had," I love them all dearly.

*****

Sweetheart, I began my memoirs with you, and I want to end them with you. You and I have spent a major part of our lives together. We have lived and loved, laughed and cried, struggled and won, suffered and overcome many things in our lives. You lost so much in your life, and I tried to make up for it. We never lost faith in each other, never had to regret anything, because our love for each other was strong and lasted until death parted us … for better or worse … I still love you, my sweetheart, and I miss you so much.

*****

Anecdotes and other stories from a time in my life before I met Lloyd, or when he was uninvolved:

While I was a student at the teachers college in Feldkirch, I took on several different summer school jobs. As a future teacher, I volunteered to work in children's summer holiday camps in Vorarlberg for two weeks at a time during the summer holidays in 1949 and 1950.

During the school year of 1951, I knitted a lovely jacket for the renowned Benger textile company: the main body I made of light gray cotton and decorated the rim with white and yellow stripes the whole way around. My jacket was exhibited at the Benger exhibition stand during the yearly fair in Dornbirn. At the end of the exhibition, the management thanked me and gave me the jacket as a gift.

*****

Our mathematics professor knew of my parents' tight financial situation; after all, restorers of antiques and old paintings—my father's profession—hardly found work after

World War II. Our professor saw the need and arranged for me to be awarded a scholarship by the local state government for the last two years in college. I no longer had to travel daily from Bludenz to Feldkirch and find places to get a lunch, as I could live in the college's boarding house. In my first three years at the college, I had received a luncheon invitation every Wednesday from the local Catholic home economics school. The parents of one of my classmates invited me to lunch on two days a week. One of my classmates was on good terms with the cook of the boarding school. Her mother gave her foodstuff to prepare a lunch in that kitchen for her and sometimes for me as well.

In the summer of 1951 a classmate helped me find paid work in the canning company Scana in Schaan, Liechtenstein. My father had a studio there, where I could sleep. I bicycled forty-five kilometers from there to Bludenz every Saturday at two in the afternoon and back to Schaan on Sunday evening. A truck took us workers to the vegetable fields to pick beans and so forth. When we worked in the fields, either we were paid by the number of full baskets we delivered at the end of a day, or we received a flat fee for the fulfillment of a set quota. At registration in the company, I was asked for my name and address. *Gassner* is a Swiss family name—my ancestors had migrated from the Canton Wallis to Vorarlberg in the fifteenth century—and I gave my father's address in Schaan. I assume I was considered to be a citizen of Liechtenstein. In the second week of working there, I was called into the office and asked for my citizenship. As a presumed citizen of Liechtenstein due to my name and address, I was paid 90 rappen (0.9 Swiss Francs), while an Austrian received only 70 rappen per hour for working in the fields or in the factory, harvesting veggies from seven in the morning until two in the afternoon and then preparing veggies for canning until six in the evening. In the office, I was asked for my citizenship ... and my wage was correspondingly reduced to 70 rappen. I was one of the few foreigners who worked on Saturdays until two in the afternoon—after all I slept in Liechtenstein. On those mornings, I had to prepare apricots for canning. An overseer noticed that I cut the apricots better than any other worker. So I was sent to a special room, where I had a chair to sit and work. Besides, that room was not wet, while the floor of the large workroom, where all the other workers did their jobs, was covered with water, sometimes one centimeter deep and more. Once all the apricots were finished, I received a single can of fruit as a premium for my exact work.

*****

In the college, we had a professor of pedagogy, whose wife taught us German and also French as an elective. I studied French with her for two years. The professor owned a hotel in the Semmering mountain area in Lower Austria. In the second half of my summer holidays in 1952, I became quite ill and spent a few weeks in a hospital in the Montafon valley. On discharge, my parents were advised to send me away for a few weeks to restore my health. This professor and his wife invited me to spend that time in their hotel, as high season was over, and they had plenty of space. There I saw the first Russians in my life, soldiers of the Allied occupation forces. Every evening they sang in their camp between Payerbach and Gloggnitz. I enjoyed their singing very much and admired their deep basses and high tenors. Their music instilled in me my love for Russian choirs and Russian voices in general. At the same time I became interested in Russian literature. Over the years I read Tolstoy, Dostoyevsky, Gorky, Pushkin, Turgenev, Chekhov, Pasternak, and eventually Solzhenitsyn. I helped in the hotel and, time permitting, went on many beautiful walks in the Semmering forests and in the Rax mountains.

In 1954 our studies at the teachers college came to an end. It is traditional in Austria to go as a whole class on a one-week trip. We chose a bus trip around Austria with an overnight stop at our professor's hotel. From then on for the next four years, I spent about seven weeks of my summer holidays in that hotel to help, wherever help was needed. There I dived into a long lost world, the world of aristocracy. Most guests stayed there for at least four weeks, many of them having been aristocrats prior to World War I. In 1919, aristocracy was abolished in Austria, and many aristocrats were disowned, and, of course, all of them had lost their aristocratic titles. However, as this hotel had, prior to World War I, mostly served aristocratic guests, and many of them were old now and homesick for "the good old days," they returned to "their" hotel, once the Russians had left Austria in the spring of 1955. I was instructed how to address our guests and how to behave in their presence. Soon I began to enjoy their company.

Now three episodes I still remember vividly. Count Thun and his wife, Else Wohlgemuth, a famous actress of the Burgtheater in Vienna, as well as Count Kielmansegg, occupied rooms on the second floor. One early morning, Count Thun came to the kitchen with his wife's little dog in his arms to tell me that he had to take a taxi to

Vienna immediately, because the little darling could not walk anymore and needed to be seen by his veterinary doctor. After lamenting the bad luck, I asked Hermi, our waitress, to order a taxi, and soon the count was off. I continued preparing breakfasts, when Hermi approached me in excitement and told me that she could not bring the breakfast to the count's wife, because the door was locked and Else Wohlgemuth did not open it. However, she heard her whining. I dashed up to the second floor and asked her what was wrong. She told me that she had slipped on the always superbly polished parquet and was lying on the floor unable to get up. I took the longest ladder, climbed up from outside, pushed the window open, and saw the problem. I called Dr. Artner, the village doctor, who got very excited to be called to this famous actress, and told his wife, one of her great admirers, to dress in a Red Cross uniform and go with him. It would be her only chance to see the actress so close. An ambulance was called, and she was taken to the hospital in Wiener Neustadt, accompanied by the doctor and his wife. She had broken her left upper arm and was kept in the hospital. The count returned with the little dog sometime in the afternoon. Upon hearing what had happened to his beloved wife, he put his doggie into my arms and went to the hospital by taxi again. In the evening he returned and thanked me with the very first box of chocolates I had ever received.

The Duchess von and zu Hohenlohe and her son, Prince von and zu Hohenlohe, lived on the top floor and expected a cocoa and a croissant every afternoon at four o'clock. I had to address them as "Your Excellency" and "Your Honor." One day as I entered their room with their afternoon snacks, one of the croissants slipped off the plate and landed near the prince's feet. The wooden floors in the hotel were always polished spick-and-span. I apologized and picked it up. It looked still as fresh as from the bakery. Now, what shall I do? Walk all the way down four flights of steps, then along the rather long corridor to the kitchen for a new one? I seated myself on the top of the steps, somewhat angry at the slippery floors, when suddenly I realized that those two had been the last croissants. What could I bring them instead? I did what was logical …

Ritter von Liszt was in his eighties when he and his wife were guests in the hotel. They stayed for eight weeks and wanted an account every fortnight. Tante Lotte, the hotel owner's aunt, gave me the account to present it to him on a silver plate. He looked at it and declared that this was not his account. I scrutinized it and ventured to say that it was correct. He got angry and told me that one of his eight titles was missing! I apologized and returned to Tante Lotte. She was Italian by birth—and I do not want to repeat her comment. She checked his registration and found the missing title. A new account was written, and I delivered it to him again. He counted his titles, and the bill was accepted. By the way, the title "Ritter von …" was originally given to the composer Franz Liszt, who did not want it and passed it on to his brother, whose son was dead set to use it in this hotel. After my time in the hotel, Tante Lotte took me to the State Opera in Vienna. While I was enraptured by the performance, she fell asleep and snored. I had to wake her up to go home.

*****

In 1958, I got in touch with a youth travel organization called OEKISTA that had an office in Innsbruck. I was chosen to accompany and look after twenty Austrian children in a camp in Cesenatico, Italy, for three weeks. In total, we were about two hundred children between eight and fourteen years and enough counselors to look after them and still have a day off every week. When I went there for the second time, on our free day, three of us counselors hitchhiked south to see more of Italy. Among other drivers, Attilio Brunori, a *brigadiere di polizzia*, who was on his way to Rome, gave us a lift. He stopped the car quite often and bought us coffee, sometimes with, other times without, a dash of cognac in it. He could speak English very well and told us of his having been a partisan in Mussolini's army and of his imprisonment by the British army in Alexandria, Egypt. He dropped us off in Ancona. Walking along the sidewalk there, I suddenly collapsed and landed on the ground. When I regained consciousness, I noticed a lot of noisy Italians hovering over me, shouting advice about what should be done about me. I also became aware that I was very wet. Suddenly a shopkeeper appeared and poured a bucket of water over me, I now understood why I was so wet. My camp companions were relieved to see me "alive" again and decided that we would hitchhike back to Cesenatico straightaway. There I consulted the camp doctor, who told me off about drinking so many cups of coffee with cognac and warned me that I could have died or at least gotten serious heart problems.

The third time I took work in the camp, I was the camp director. On the way back to Innsbruck, I had a girl with a bad sore throat and a slight fever in my train compartment.

Suddenly, I heard the customs officials in the corridor. O god; I had bought far too many things for my family and myself to get through customs without a problem. So when they opened the door and asked me if I had anything to declare, instead of answering their question, I closed the door halfway and told them that I had a very sick child with me who could possibly have diphtheria. They immediately left … and I was saved.

*****

I have not only got amusing stories to tell. My next and, as far as these memoirs are concerned, last two memorable occurrences in my life turned out to be rather dangerous. In retrospect, I wonder whether I was so naïve or self-assured or courageous to put myself politically on slippery grounds in Bulgaria and in East Germany during the communist times. For several years, I had wanted to meet Professor Lozanov, whose research in suggestology had fascinated me. I had seen videos of him lecturing and his master teacher, Evelina Gateva, practicing suggestopedic teaching. On one of my private visits with my husband to Vienna in the mid-1980s I found out that the Austrian and the Bulgarian governments had concluded a cultural exchange agreement. I immediately thought that a visit to Sofia would now be much easier than before. The Ministries of Foreign Affairs and of Education each issued me a letter to take along to Bulgaria. My cousin Edith offered to take care of Lloyd, while I would have meetings with Professor Lozanov and his master teacher. Upon arrival at the airport in Sofia, I was told that I had to stay in the Hemus hotel. I shared a taxi with a German and a French tourist. Those two people were taken to two different hotels in the city, and I was driven out of the city to my hotel. I asked the driver why I could not stay in a city hotel. His answer was "Orders." My fairly large hotel was full of Russians. In the afternoon I walked to Lozanov's institute, not expecting any problems; after all, I had two letters from two ministries in Vienna. As I reached the front door, three young men dressed in jeans surrounded me and asked me what I wanted. I pulled out my two ministerial letters, smiled and told them that I had written to Professor Lozanov, who expected me to give him my research papers and discuss them with him. The men spoke German quite well and informed me that neither Lozanov nor Gateva were in the building. They asked me to give them my papers. I refused and said that I would wait until I could speak with them. Then I opened the door, and they let me enter. A Maria came, showed me a seat, and confirmed that the people I wanted to see were not there; they were probably in Russia. I did not believe a word, smiled, and insisted on waiting for them. Every so often she passed me and repeated what she had already told me. Still, I was convinced that she was lying. In those days, Lozanov's work was politically very sensitive and had aroused great interest in the West. After a few hours, Gateva stormed out of a room opposite my chair. Shortly thereafter, Lozanov appeared accompanied by a guard. I jumped up to greet him and give him my papers, but, surprisingly, he could speak neither English nor German. However, on the videos I had watched, he could speak both these languages. His guard asked me to give him my papers, but I refused. After a few minutes of trying to communicate with each other, Lozanov was taken away, and I left the institute somewhat bewildered. I walked into the city, ate something, and then found a streetcar that brought me back to my hotel. At half past one in the morning, my telephone rang, and a voice with a strong Bulgarian accent asked me, "Wann verlassen Sie Bulgarien?" (When are you going to leave Bulgaria?) I got scared and could not answer; instead I hung up. In the morning, I took a streetcar to the Austrian Embassy—I had asked my first driver from the day of my arrival where the embassy was, and he drove by it upon my request. There I told a secretary my story. He passed it on to the ambassadress. The secretary returned with the message that a "mole" would be sent out to investigate what was going on. I was advised to be careful. In the afternoon, I tried again to meet with Lozanov but in vain. I was not allowed to enter the building. In the hotel, I wanted to book a ticket for a folkloristic evening; later I asked to be allowed to visit the Rila Monasteries, but to all my requests, I received a foul negative answer. My return flight was on Saturday, so I still had three days left to entertain myself. What should I do? I went to the wonderful Orthodox Nevsky Cathedral and visited an exhibition of the one hundred most beautiful icons of the Orthodox churches. On entering, I had to show my ticket to an old woman. Because of her age, I assumed that she might speak German, and she did! Viennese German with a heavy Bulgarian accent. She almost cried talking to me and became abrupt the moment another person was in sight. The icons were so exquisite that I spent several hours in the basement of that cathedral, where the exhibition was laid out. Unfortunately, I had no further opportunity to talk to the old woman again. The next morning, I visited a church similar to the church near the Kreml in Moscow.

There I attended an Orthodox service, where the choir sang so movingly that I cried. I still find Slavic voices/choirs heartrending. Once I wanted a good lunch and ordered my meal in the Hotel Bulgaria. The waiter brought me a large menu with a big selection of dishes, written also in English and French. I chose my meal, but when the waiter returned, he declared, "Today we have schnitzel." The schnitzel turned out to be a greasy hamburger! I knew that I was being followed on the streets, even when I entered shops to buy some souvenirs such as a mocca service for six and LPs with the world-renowned Bulgarian opera bass singer Boris Christoff, whom I had heard in Verdi's *Don Carlo* sing King Philip II at Covent Garden, while I lived in London. I spent a considerable amount of time simply walking in the city and observing the people. One afternoon, I came across the mausoleum of Georgi Dimitrow, the founder of the Bulgarian communist party. It was an impressive building made of marble similar to the Lenin Mausoleum in Moscow, constructed in August 1969. Hundreds of people were queuing up to get in. I joined them, hoping my visit there would put my "observer," and with him the Bulgarian government, into a better mood about me. I noticed many country people in the queue. At almost every couple of meters a guard in uniform urged the visitors to move on. One was not allowed to pause anywhere, least of all at the glass sarcophagus where his embalmed body rested. This building was destroyed, against the will of the majority of the Bulgarian population, in August 1999. Three attempts were made to break it down, but a fourth was needed to get it to crumble.

Every night, always at half past one, I was woken up by the phone call about my departure. On Friday night, I yelled into the phone, "You know exactly when I will leave this country; stop bothering me!" Early the following morning, someone from the Austrian Embassy rang and urged me to leave Bulgaria as quickly as possible. That morning I only got a small cup of coffee and a piece of bread for breakfast, no hard-boiled egg, no butter, no jam. I had to sit alone at a very small table in a corner of the restaurant; all other tables were occupied by Russians. That was the moment when I got really scared. I packed my travel bag, paid my bill, and left. My passport had been held back at the airport upon my arrival. I took a streetcar to the Japanese hotel, which was situated only a few stops away from my hotel, and sat there in the lobby until shortly before midday, reading German and English newspapers. Two of them I packed into my bag. A taxi took me to the airport. The ground stewardess issued me a boarding card, when a woman appeared. She seemed to be quite friendly and asked me how much money I had, what I had done with the obligatory Leva—tourists had to exchange a certain amount of money for Bulgarian Lewa after arrival at the airport. Then she took my wallet and my boarding card and led me into a room, locking the door behind her. There I sat, getting more and more worried, without a drink of water or the possibility to use a toilet and nothing to read—a worse situation than in a prison. Shortly before five in the evening, I saw my airplane arrive and passengers leaving, then others boarding. Suddenly the "friendly" woman opened the door and, with a smile on her face, returned my passport, my wallet, and my boarding card, saying, "You forgot your documents!" A man led me to the plane, and I got on, promising myself never to set foot on Bulgarian soil again. Today the situation is, of course, very different, so that I would like to revisit the remarkable places I had seen in Sofia.

*****

As mentioned earlier in these memoirs, during the communist years I traveled to the GDR (East Germany) several times either for research purposes or to conferences. East Berlin, Dresden, and Leipzig were my destinations. In East Berlin, my co-researcher and I once walked along Köpenicker Straße, when I noticed something that looked to me like an electric transformer. I asked my companion what it was. He answered, "You and your activities are registered there like everybody else's." Further on along the same road I expressed my interest in a very large mansion-type building, standing in a large park and watched by a uniformed guard with a gun in his hands. The answer to my question was "Didn't you notice that there are no invalid or old people in the streets of Berlin? In this building there live those Berliners we don't want on the streets." I was shocked.

On a big square in the centre of Dresden, my eyes detected kindergarten teachers pushing carts with up to six children under four years of age and with a small table in the middle, three children sitting on either side and two children holding on to the sides of the carts. I took a photo and shook my head somewhat bewildered. When I was in the train to Leipzig at another time, one passenger began a conversation with me, once the other passenger had left the train in Eisenach. I mentioned my observation in Dresden to him, and he explained to me, "After the age of seven months, our children have to be put into a *hort* (all-day kindergarten) so that both parents can go to work to help build up our country from the damages inflicted on it during World War II. The parents see their offspring only from evening to morning." He identified himself as the chief pediatrician of Saxony. Additionally, he said that taking children so early in their lives away from their parents was, in his opinion, the reason why there were so many neurotic children in the GDR. He could not have said these things safely had another passenger been in the compartment.

On my last visit to Leipzig, where I observed suggestopedic lessons in Cuban Spanish, a very good-looking, tall, blond, and blue-eyed man in his thirties offered to drive me in his Lada to the Hotel Leipzig, where I stayed during my visit to the institute. On my last day there, he invited me to drive with him to Berlin, because he wanted me to see the Peace Palace there. I expressed my interest but told him that my visa allowed me only to stay in the city of Leipzig. He assured me that I could travel with him anywhere in the GDR. Well, I "heard" warning signals in my brain. He offered me a yearly flight ticket from Australia to Berlin, if I joined the East German-Australian Society. More warning signals! Of course, I would get free accommodation in Berlin whenever I visited there. I began to feel uneasy. After he had dropped me off at my hotel, I called my co-researcher, and we arranged a meeting in a teahouse near the St. Thomas church. I wished to tell him what had happened, but he stopped me and led me out of the city and into a field, where we could talk freely. He urged me to leave Leipzig that same evening, and I did. Once back in Adelaide, I entrusted this experience to Brian, our chairman, and we arranged that if someone from the GDR should visit our department and ask for me, I would be "interstate" and therefore unavailable. It happened … and I left the building via the staircase, not using the lift, which was almost opposite the secretariat. A few months later, the Berlin Wall came down.

*****

I have now come to the end of my memoirs, although I would have more happenings to share. To tell my life's story has several reasons: I wrote it for my husband to express my unending love for him, to remember the wonderful but short time we had in good health, to let the reader know what a loving caregiver can do for the loved one and for one's own self, to give courage to the patient as well as to encourage one's own self, to recognize the power of music versus tranquillizers, and to *not give up* before the time has come to go. We need physicians, but we also need the *love* and *care* of our partner, family, or friend. More than a third of my life I shared with my very sick and subsequently sometimes difficult husband. I am satisfied and happy that I did it and that I managed to combine caring and my professional career.

Writing these memoirs has been therapeutic for me. If someone like me in my situation needs advice or help, one has to look for it and not be too proud or ashamed of asking for help. For a while, I consulted an elderly psychiatrist in Australia whose husband lost his memory at the age of thirty-six. She shared with me her wisdom of age, her professional knowledge, and her practical experience, all of which I am thankful for. Here in Austria, I speak to my young "mentor," who listens and gives me strength to cope with my life since my husband's death. He stands by me when my feelings overwhelm me while remembering and reliving my past. He encourages me to recognize and accept my emotions as part of

my life's story, as difficult as that may be. One's ratio and emotio
are often far apart. It is hard work to bring them together to reach
a balance, but one must do it. By writing these memoirs, I lifted
the burden of my life, and I got to know myself better.

In good or bad times, in sickness or health,
love wins.

Acknowledgments

My thanks for sharing their ideas with me and their help throughout my life go to many of my friends and acquaintances in Europe, America, and Australia. Without their assistance over many years, writing these memoirs would not have been possible.

In particular, I wish to thank my friend and lector Sally Schreiber. We spent many hours together fine-tuning the text of these memoirs.

Furthermore, I am most thankful to my mentor, Dr. André Piuk, without whose most sensitive psychological guidance I would not have been able to go through my life mentally again and share it with whomever will read these memoirs.

In memoriam, I owe thanks to Dr. Bronte Pulsford, who helped me psychologically in the early stages of Lloyd's illness. Without her deep understanding of my situation and the resulting problems, I might not have been able to cope with caring for my husband and at the same time fulfilling my professional duties.

Printed in the United States
By Bookmasters